SUMMER-BLOOMING
BULBS

Scores of Spectacular Bloomers
for Your Summer Garden

Beth Hanson-Editor

Above: blackberry lily, *Belamcanda chinensis.*
Cover: tiger flower, *Tigridia pavonia.*

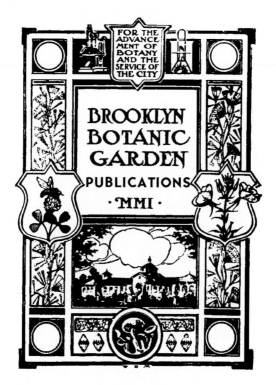

Janet Marinelli
SERIES EDITOR

Sigrun Wolff Saphire
ASSOCIATE EDITOR

Mark Tebbitt
SCIENCE EDITOR

Anne Garland
ART DIRECTOR

Steven Clemants
VICE-PRESIDENT, SCIENCE & PUBLICATIONS

Judith D. Zuk
PRESIDENT

Elizabeth Scholtz
DIRECTOR EMERITUS

Handbook #169
Copyright © 2001 by the Brooklyn Botanic Garden, Inc.
Handbooks in the *21st-Century Gardening Series,* formerly *Plants & Gardens,*
are published quarterly at 1000 Washington Ave., Brooklyn, NY 11225.
Subscription included in Brooklyn Botanic Garden subscriber membership dues ($35.00 per year).
ISBN # 1-889538-23-X
Printed by Science Press, a division of the Mack Printing Group.
Printed on recycled paper.

TABLE OF CONTENTS

INTRODUCTION

SUMMER-BLOOMING BULBS

BETH HANSON

I RECENTLY FOUND MYSELF at a local nursery rooting through several bins filled with bizarrely shaped brown lumps, some of which looked and felt a lot like old leather gardening gloves that had spent the winter in the compost pile. But this was the summer-bulb display, and these humble lumps are the source of some of the most spectacular blossoms and dramatic foliage of summer. To be botanically accurate, not all of these are true bulbs; some are corms, tubers, or rhizomes. These plants, which store the nutrients they need for their annual renewal and begin their growth underground, are known as "geophytes" (literally translated: "earth plants"). That many originate in the tropical and subtropical regions of the world is obvious: The boldly striped cannas, beach-umbrella-sized elephant ears, pineapple-shaped eucomises, and ginger lilies sporting flame-colored, torchlike blossoms can't deny their striking tropical heritage. But summer bulbs also shade into more subtle hues and forms: the delicately scented, pale pink flowers of ×*Amarcrinum memoria-corsii*, the ethereal Chinese ground orchid, the lavender-blue clusters of flowers of the blue dicks, which sway in the breeze on wiry stems. Leaf through the "Encyclopedia of Summer-blooming Bulbs" starting on page 49 and you will get a sense of their extensive range.

Come summer, the bizarrely shaped lumps on the right give rise to beautiful flowers like the dahlias on the left.

Most of these bulbs are tender north of Zone 5 and won't survive cold winters, but the variety, adaptability, and extended blooming time of these plants may make it worth nursing them through the winter indoors in colder areas. You'll have to dig up the bulbs around the date of the first frost and store them through their dormant season in a cool spot in slightly damp peat moss, then plant them out in the garden or a pot the following spring. Or it may even be worthwhile to use the less costly of these plants as annuals, replacing them year after year.

In addition to the encyclopedia, this volume provides lots more guidance on summer bulbs, starting with an introduction to their botanical features. Read on and you will learn how to care for these plants throughout the year, from planting to winter storage. You'll find tips on how to incorporate them into beds and borders with more familiar garden plants to show them off to best effect, as well as how to grow them in containers. You'll also learn how to propagate them and how to prevent and manage pests and diseases using the least toxic remedies available.

If you've never ventured into the world of bulbs beyond the ubiquitous daffodils, tulips, and crocuses of spring, this book is a call to action: Get bold! If it's spring as you read this, take a trip to your local garden center and check out the selection; or for a wider assortment, turn to the list of mail-order sources at the back of the book. Many nurseries now have web sites, where you can click through a multitude of photos. If it's fall or winter, kick back and fantasize about the amazing collages of textures, colors, and scents you'll be able to create when you begin weaving summer bulbs into your garden.

A few summer-flowering bulbs, such as lilies and Japanese iris above, have graced gardens for decades.

A BUYER'S GUIDE TO BULBS: WHAT GARDENERS CAN DO TO PROTECT THREATENED SPECIES

Most of us perceive gardening as an environmentally benign, even beneficial pastime. Little do we suspect that bulbs purchased locally and subsequently planted in a backyard bed may have been harvested from unmanaged and possibly fragile wild populations thousands of miles away. When bulbs, corms, rhizomes, and other plant parts are collected from wild spaces in exotic places to supply ornamental, floral, and medicinal markets, sensitive species and entire ecosystems may be put at risk. Whether bulbs were gathered from the wild or propagated in a nursery may not be obvious at first glance, but rules on labeling have made it easier to find out. Gardeners can have a positive influence on bulb conservation by asking appropriate questions and making responsible purchasing decisions.

U.S. Government guidelines, established by the Federal Trade Commission, advise the nursery industry against selling plants collected from wild sources without disclosing this fact to consumers. Vendors should not use the term *nursery-grown* when selling plant material of wild origin. However, nurseries may label plants descended from those lawfully collected from wild populations as *nursery-propagated*. Similarly, bulbs sold by the Netherlands, the largest bulb producer and exporter, to the United States or any other country must bear a label that identifies them as either "Bulbs from wild source" or "Bulbs grown from cultivated stock." This clarification is important because it ensures that wild-harvested bulbs that are shipped to the Netherlands and subsequently exported from there are clearly and accurately labeled.

Consumers can also take comfort in knowing that many species at risk from international trade are regulated by more than 150 countries (including the United States and Canada) belonging to the Convention on International Trade in Endangered Species. CITES is the primary mechanism to directly regulate trade in flora and fauna at the international level. Depending on the level of endangerment from international trade or other threats, plant and animal species are listed in one of three appendices (I, II, III). Species listed in Appendix I are threatened with extinction and may not be commercially traded unless they are nursery-propagated, which qualifies them for Appendix II. The majority of plant species regulated by CITES are listed in Appendix II, under which plants can be commercially traded provided government approval and export permits are granted. Three bulb genera are currently listed in CITES Appendix II: *Cyclamen*, *Galanthus,* and *Sternbergia*. In Appendix III, individual countries unilaterally decide to list native species that are exported and for which they seek greater domestic protection. For more information on CITES and species listed in its appendices, check out www.cites.org.

When faced with ambiguous labeling, do not hesitate to ask retailers to clarify the origin of bulbs and give preference to bulbs known to have been nursery-propagated or collected from carefully managed wild stock.

—Christopher S. Robbins

BULBOUS BOTANY

STEVEN E. CLEMANTS

BOTANISTS ARE NOTORIOUS for changing the names of plants, but they are very precise about the use of descriptive terms such as *bulb*. To a gardener, a bulb is any perennial that overwinters as a fleshy underground structure. To a botanist, bulb means something much more specific: A true bulb is a fleshy underground bud. It is not a corm, rhizome, tuber, or tuberous root (root tuber), all of which gardeners group together loosely as bulbs; these non-bulbs are in fact swollen roots or stems.

The botanical term for the gardener's bulb is "geophyte," literally "earth plant"—a term coined by Christien Raunkiaer. The Danish botanist devised a classification system based on the location of a plant's dormant buds, and thus where new growth occurs. In geophytes, new growth begins below ground,

Like the gladioli seen here in their native habitat in South Africa, most ornamental bulbs are native to the so-called Mediterranean regions of the world.

Bulbous plants like these spider lilies have food reserves that enable them to endure harsh conditions, then bloom rapidly when the weather is right.

while in other perennial plants new growth occurs at or above ground level. In this chapter, *geophyte* refers to the gardener's bulb and *bulb* refers to the botanist's bulb. In other chapters, the term "bulb" will be used more loosely.

WHERE GEOPHYTES GROW

Geophytes come from almost every corner of the globe, but many of the ornamental species are found in regions with hot, dry summers and cool, wet winters. For example, many alliums and tulips come from the Mediterranean basin (extending east through Iran and Turkey to China); *Camassia quamash* and *Triteleia laxa* are native to California; *Oxalis magellanica* and several *Hippeastrum* species come from Chile; *Agapanthus*, Cape lilies (*Crinum* species) and most of the cultivated *Gladiolus* come from southern Africa. A number of less frequently cultivated species are found in western and southern Australia. Geophytes often have an advantage in these climates because they store their food during relatively short growing seasons and survive the long dry seasons as the storage organs.

SPRING AND SUMMER BLOOMERS

Geophytes can be separated further by the season when they flower. The most common are spring-flowering and summer-flowering types, though autumn- and winter-flowering geophytes do occur. Most spring-flowering geophytes, also known as hardy geophytes, are planted in the fall, flower in the spring, will shed their foliage by summer, and can stay in the ground over the winter. They originate in temperate areas of the world and include tulips, irises, and crocuses, for example. Most summer-flowering geophytes, also known as tender geophytes, are planted in the spring and flower in the summer, and in areas with cold winters, the storage organ—the bulb, corm, tuber, or rhizome—must be removed in the fall and stored indoors until spring. These summer-flowering forms generally originate in tropical and subtropical regions.

TYPES OF GEOPHYTES

It's useful to know how to distinguish the different types of geophytes from fibrous-rooted plants and from each other because this will help you determine how to plant them. One of the most common ways to tell them apart is to group them according to where they store the starches and sugars for food.

Bulb

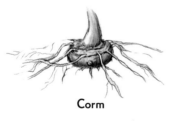

Corm

Rhizome

What gardeners call bulbs are geophytes or "earth plants" to botanists, who differentiate between bulbs, corms, rhizomes, stem tubers, and root tubers depending on where the plants store their food reserves.

BULBS

A true bulb is really just a typical shoot compressed into a shortened form. Food is stored in a number of small, fleshy "scale" leaves. Most bulbs are more or less egg-shaped, with a stem "plate" at the wider end. Attached to this stem are the storage leaves, forming concentric circles surrounding the growing tip. (If you cut a bulb in two horizontally, you'll see the concentric rings typical of an onion cut in half.) From the lower part of the stem new roots form, growing downward. So it's important to plant the bulb with this broader, root-forming end facing down. Many of the commonly cultivated geophytes are bulbs, including amaryllises, alliums, and lilies.

CORMS

In a corm, food is stored in the stem tissue. Many corms look a lot like bulbs because they often have the same egg shape. But if you cut a corm in half, you'll see that it does not have the concentric rings of fleshy leaves that bulbs have. Instead, it is one mass of homogeneous tissue—this is stem tissue. In both bulbs and corms, roots grow from the wider end, and therefore a corm should be

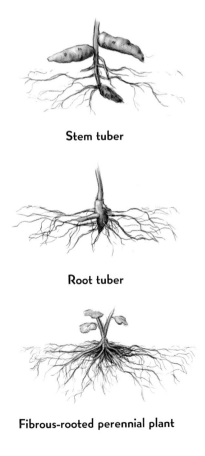

Stem tuber

Root tuber

In geophytes, new growth always begins below ground, whereas in other perennial plants, like the fibrous-rooted specimen shown at right, new growth begins at or above ground level.

Fibrous-rooted perennial plant

11

planted with the wide side facing down. Buds poke out of the pointy end. Gladioli and freesias are corms.

RHIZOMES

In rhizomes, as in corms, food is stored in the stem. Indeed, *rhizome* is a general term for a stem growing more or less horizontally below ground level, so you should plant rhizomes horizontally. Rhizomes tend to be thick, and fleshy or woody, and bear nodes with small, thin, generally non-photosynthesizing leaves (scale leaves) and buds. Growth occurs at the buds on the ends of the rhizome or nearby nodes. You can distinguish rhizomes from roots by the presence of scale leaves or scars where old leaves have fallen off. Irises and cannas are rhizomes.

STEM TUBERS

As their name implies, these plants, like the two described above, store food in the stem. It's often hard to tell a stem tuber from a rhizome; they're both swollen, horizontal, usually underground stems. But stem tubers usually form at the ends of a rhizome and will give rise to new rhizomes at the end of the following year.

Top: True bulbs, such as chinks (*Ornithogalum saundersiae*), store food in a number of fleshy "scale" leaves.
Bottom: In a corm like this gladiolus, food is stored as a homogeneous mass in the stem tissue.

Growth starts from one or more nodes or buds called "eyes" at the base of the older stem. Like rhizomes, stem tubers should be planted horizontally, with at least one growing eye attached to each division. The potato is the most easily recognized stem tuber, but some anemones and cannas produce them as well.

ROOT TUBERS
Root tubers are swollen roots in which food is stored. Because they are roots, they lack nodes, leaf scars, and buds. Root tubers must include a portion of the stem with one or more buds to be viable. This portion of the stem is usually planted facing upward. Dahlias are the best-known root tubers; gloriosa lilies are another example.

THE LIFE CYCLES OF GEOPHYTES

You must understand a plant's life cycle to grow and care for it successfully. Armed with this knowledge, you will know when to water your plants, when to withhold water, and when to repot and begin watering again to coax them back into bloom.

Geophytes, whether bulbs, corms, tubers, or rhizomes, have one thing in common: They have a dormant period. During adverse weather—either hot and dry summers or cold and snowy winters—many geophytes shed their foliage and live off nutrients stored up during favorable conditions. "Dormant" is really a misnomer for this phase: Though they appear to be resting, most geophytes continue to develop, but the changes take place out of sight, underground, fueled by food stored during the previous growing season. Geophytes are best transplanted at this time when they do not require light or water.

When environmental conditions once again become favorable for growth, the plant is stimulated to put out roots, leaves, and flowers. Many geophytes adapted to survive the winter cold respond to a rise in temperature; those adapted to lie low in hot and dry conditions are attuned to an increase in moisture. Moreover, geophytes are tuned finely enough that they will usually not respond to just any rise in temperature or increase in moisture—a freak warm spell in December or a rain shower in July won't get a rise out of the properly conditioned geophyte. This mechanism protects them from sending out vulnerable shoots that would be killed off when more typical seasonal weather again prevails.

Geophytes often start their growing season with a rush, producing flowers and leaves at the same time or sometimes producing flowers before leaves. This effort usually exhausts the geophyte's store of nutrients, and the plant either dies after fruiting or attempts to accumulate enough nutrients for the next flowering season. For this reason, you should not cut off the leaves after flowering; they are working to build up food stores through photosynthesis.

Some dry-climate species (amaryllises, for example) may keep growing if you don't simulate the drought spell they would experience in their native habitats, but they probably will never produce flowers. Stop watering after the plant has had a chance to build up its food reserves, and let it rest for a few months. 🎋

YEAR-ROUND CARE OF SUMMER BULBS

BECKY AND BRENT HEATH

PEOPLE OFTEN EXPECT all bulbs to look just like those of daffodils and tulips—hard, round, and brown. However, many bulbs that flower in summer are not true bulbs, but rather rhizomes, tubers, corms, or root tubers, and they have odd, asymmetrical shapes and are rarely rock hard. In fact, they look more like bare-root perennials than true bulbs; but unlike perennials, these bulbs produce a sometimes funny-looking nutrient storage chamber that gives them a head-start on the growing season and allows them to be safely out of the ground for a short period of time. When buying bulbs, inspect them closely and avoid or return any with soft, brown, mushy spots, as these may be infected with an insect pest or a disease. For best success, plant the bulbs as soon as possible.

STARTING TENDER BULBS INDOORS

If you're gardening in an area that's colder than the USDA zones recommended for certain tender bulbs, you can still grow them, but you may want to start them in pots indoors. This will enable the plants to develop and mature early enough to give you a long season of enjoyment. Once the weather has warmed, you can transplant them into the garden or simply drop them with their pots into decorative containers. Enjoy the potted plants on your deck or patio all summer long, then move them back indoors in the fall. Winter care may vary, so consult the cultural instructions for each bulb.

To start tender bulbs indoors, plant them in pots at the recommended depth and place them about 6 to 12 inches below grow lights to keep the plants from becoming leggy, which can happen as the foliage stretches upward searching for light. In addition, place a Gro-Mat, Heat Mat, food warming tray, or similar device under the pots to give them bottom heat of about 70° F. Most tropical bulbs love warm soils and hate to be cold. They will root best and have the showiest blooms if they are grown in soils between 65° and 75° F. Exposure to cold early in their development can stress bulbs and make them more susceptible to fungus problems and rotting, or may even cause them to abort their blooms.

PLANTING OUTDOORS

Amending your garden soil is the key to making your bulbs thrive. They may emerge if planted in almost any soil, from clay to sand, but they probably won't flourish unless the soil contains the proper nutrients and enough organic matter, and provides adequate drainage. We've added organic matter to our soil for many years, and with each passing year, we believe more strongly in its benefits. When planted in organically

Like cannas, most tropical bulbs love warm soils, so gardeners in colder areas may want to start them indoors and move them out once the soil has warmed.

enriched soil, our plants are healthier, taller, and lusher, require less care and water, and produce more flowers.

Before planting, add lots of well-decomposed organic matter to your soil—compost, leaves, horse manure, or anything else that will enrich the soil and provide unrefined nutrients. It's best to do this before planting: Till a 2- to 6-inch layer of organic matter into the soil; in subsequent years, top-dress hardy bulbs with a 1- to 2-inch layer while the bulbs are dormant.

If you have an area in your garden with no actively growing plants, you can easily plant a large number of bulbs at once: Just lay down a thick layer of compost and place the bulbs right on top; then cover the bulbs with sand, soil, or mulch to the proper depth. This is an easy way to plant bulbs in a raised bed, which will improve drainage and add organic matter, ensuring that the bulbs are in good soil.

Hardy summer bulbs like lilies, lilies-of-the-valley, and alstroemerias can be

For gorgeous blooms and healthy plants, add lots of organic matter to the soil before planting and top-dress hardy bulbs like lilies with a 1- to 2-inch layer of organic mulch while the bulbs are dormant.

planted as soon as the risk that the ground may freeze has passed, at about the same time you would plant peas. Plant tender bulbs like cannas, dahlias, and elephant ears later, when the soil temperature reaches at least 60° F. That's also the time to transplant any bulbs you started indoors into the garden.

Most bulbs, whether tender or hardy, will do best when planted at a depth of three times the height of the bulb. There are exceptions to this rule, so it's always best to check the cultural instructions that should be included with your bulbs. If the recommended planting depth is within a range of several inches, plant on the deeper side if you live in a cooler area, to keep the bulb below the frost line. If it's difficult to tell the top from the bottom, plant the bulb, rhizome, tuber, or corm on its side. As a rule of thumb, space bulbs about three times their width apart.

If you garden in very heavy clay soil, you may want to amend the top few inches, plant the bulbs shallower than recommended, and make up the difference in depth with a thick top-dressing of mulch, or sand and mulch. Mulch is also useful for bulbs that are only marginally hardy in your area: Top-dressing with a thick blanket (4 to 6 inches) of mulch such as pine needles, chopped leaves, or other light, airy material, can often increase a plant's hardiness by a zone or two. Just be careful not to cover the tips of the emerging leaves of bulbs, corms, rhizomes, or tubers that have begun to sprout at planting time. Instead, mulch around the leaves as they continue to grow above the surface. All of your bulbs will benefit from a mulch of any of the materials mentioned above after the soil in

In the fall, harvest tender bulbs for winter storage. Dig up the entire root system and shake off the soil.

the garden warms to about 70° F. This will conserve moisture and keep the foliage and flowers clean.

SUN AND MOISTURE CONSIDERATIONS

If you live in an area where summer temperatures are very hot, you may want to place plants that do best in full sun to partial shade in a spot that will be shaded during the hottest part of the day, from midday until afternoon. On the other hand, if you provide adequate consistent moisture, some of the bulbs mostly used in the shade (caladiums, lilies-of-the-valley, achimenes, oxalis) will tolerate full sun.

Many bulbs from tropical climates, such as caladiums and gingers, grow best in damp soils, and tend to do better when planted in soils that stay moist during the bulb's period of dormancy. Bulbs like gladioli and crocosmias, native to alpine and desert areas where soils are drier, will do best in soils that drain well and stay drier during their winter dormancy. Consequently, it is a good idea to plant these bulbs somewhat deeper than the cultural instructions suggest. Planting them in a berm or raised bed is often best.

FERTILIZING

Incorporate organic fertilizers into the soil when you're planting, then broadcast more during the growing season. If you decide to use a liquid fertilizer, reapply it every two weeks or so, depending on the amount of organic matter in your soil; liquid fertilizers tend to leach quickly through soils deficient in organic matter. In addition, it's a good idea to top-dress with a slow-release fertilizer such as Holland Bulb Booster at the time of planting and each succeeding spring to

17

maintain a good nutrient level. Just remember never to put non-organic fertilizers in the hole when you plant bulbs, as these can burn tender roots.

Most summer bulbs appreciate the extra nourishment of fertilizers, but make sure to avoid products high in nitrogen (the first number of the N-P-K fertilizer formula on the package label), as they tend to encourage lush leaf growth, sometimes at the expense of flowers. However, extra potassium (the K in the formula) is generally helpful in forming strong, disease-resistant bulbs. And phosphorus (the P) promotes strong flowering, although most soils contain sufficient amounts of this slow-moving nutrient.

In boggy areas, plants rarely will require extra fertilizer, because nutrients from the surrounding area tend to accumulate in these places along with the moisture. However, if the foliage of plants growing in a boggy area is spindly or sparse and lacks rich, dark green color, try adding 1 to 2 inches of good, well-cured compost.

SUMMER CARE

If the tired foliage of post-bloom bulbs offends you, place them among other plants to hide their fatigue among fresh growth. Don't cut back or tie up the leaves of hardy bulbs after they have bloomed: This is the time when the plants are building up nutrient stores for the following growing season. Wait to cut the foliage until it begins to turn yellow and flop over.

Allow tender bulbs to dry off after you remove them from the garden in the fall.

18

Deadhead dying flowers from plants to conserve the energy they would expend making seed, unless you have planted bulbs that naturalize (spread by seed) and you wish them to do so! Deadheading certain bulb flowers like dahlias, caladiums, anemones, cannas, and crinums will encourage them to re-bloom.

Many summer bulbs like consistent moisture, so if you live in an area where summers are dry, use drip irrigation once a week. Don't use overhead irrigation if possible, as it is hard on flowers and can foster mildew and fungal diseases.

HARVESTING AND STORING TENDER BULBS

After the leaves of tender bulbs have been killed by frost, harvest the bulbs for winter storage. Dig up the entire root system and shake off the soil, remove the dead or dying leaves close to the bulbs, and place the bulbs in dry peat moss, chipped leaves, or wood shavings in an open paper bag or container that will allow them to breathe. Store in a warm, dry place. A garage that's kept above freezing is fine.

If this process sounds too cumbersome, you can treat summer-flowering bulbs as annuals; some are less expensive than many annuals anyway. You may also be surprised to find bulbs you've written off as too tender to survive the cold will indeed come up again in spring. We're always amazed at how many summer-blooming bulbs survive the winters in our Virginia garden (Zone 7)—they seem to be far hardier than the reference books would have us all believe.

Store the bulbs for the winter in wood shavings or chipped leaves.

19

PROPAGATING BULBOUS PLANTS

ALESSANDRO CHIARI

BULBOUS PLANTS ARE EASY TO PROPAGATE, using different methods for different types of bulbs. The most common way to increase bulbous plants is vegetative, or asexual, propagation, which means propagation from a part of the plant other than its seeds. For gardeners, vegetative propagation has its advantages because it means we can be certain that all the resulting plants will be identical to the mother plant.

BULBS

During its life cycle a true bulb produces daughter bulbs called bulblets or off-sets. Before the first frost, dig out tender bulbs, separate the offsets, and store them alongside the original bulbs in a cool, dark place in dry to lightly moist peat moss, sawdust, or sand. Plant them out the following spring the same way you would plant mature flowering bulbs. Offsets of most species will need a few growing seasons to reach flowering size. Some gardeners prefer to grow off-sets in small nurseries until they are large enough to be planted in the garden. This basic method works fine for most summer bulbs.

Lilies, *Lilium* species, can also be propagated in the spring through an unusual technique called scaling. Separate the fleshy white scale leaves from the mother bulb. (This process is similar to peeling off artichoke leaves.) Insert the bottom half or third of the scale into a container filled with rooting medium, and place the container in a moist environment. For example, you can build a miniature greenhouse by putting the container into a transparent plastic bag. Eventually, small bulblets with one small leaf emerging from the soil will form at the base of the scale. Bulblets can be planted out and grown to flowering size in a few growing seasons.

You can propagate the winter-flowering *Lachenalia* from leaf cuttings: Cut well-developed leaves into sections and insert these into rooting medium. Within four to six weeks, small bulblets will appear at the base of the leaf.

Albuca and *Chasmanthe* can be propagated through bulb cuttings: Divide the bulb into four to eight vertical sections and place them in rooting medium with the top third of the bulb emerging from the medium. Bulblets will appear in

During their life cycle, true bulbs like lilies produce daughter bulbs. Separate these bulblets or offsets and in a few growing seasons they will reach flowering size.

four to six weeks, usually in between the scale leaves. Repot them or plant them out and grow them to flowering size.

CORMS

The life cycle of a true corm is not very different from that of a true bulb. Corms produce daughter corms called cormels, which you can separate from the main corm once it goes dormant. Store them as you would bulbs and bulblets. Some species of *Gladiolus* and *Ixia* produce cormels at the tip of short, slender underground stems called stolons. Make sure you follow the stolons and recover the cormels before you pull out the main corm, as the cormels detach easily from the stem.

RHIZOMES

Rhizomes are underground stems that grow horizontally. Like other stems, rhizomes branch and elongate at the growing point, the tip of each branch. Rhizomes are usually propagated through division. Cut the rhizome into sections, making sure that each one has at least one bud, or growing point. Store the rhizomes whole and divide them when it's time to plant. This prevents excessive drying and infection through the wounds. Store rhizomes as you would bulbs.

The most common way to increase bulbous plants is vegetative, or asexual, propagation, which means propagation from a part of the plant other than its seeds. Rhizomatous plants like irises, for example, are often propagated through division.

STEM TUBERS

When you divide stem tubers prior to planting, make sure that each section has at least one bud. If possible, cut the tuber two to three days prior to planting and keep the divisions in a warm, humid place to allow the wounds to seal naturally. This will prevent pathogens in the soil from colonizing the fresh cut. Stem tubers are very easy to store. Put them in a dark, cool place, and don't bother covering them with peat moss or sand. Store tropical tubers like *Caladium* at 60° F. or higher; otherwise their performance in the garden will suffer.

TUBEROUS STEMS

From a botanical point of view, a tuberous stem is an enlargement that forms at the base of the stem and near the top of the root system. This structure, commonly called a "tuber," is a unique type of stem tuber that lacks buds. Typical examples of plants with this structure are tuberous begonia, *Begonia* × *tuberhybrida*, and *Cyclamen*. The best way to propagate tuberous begonia is from stem cuttings. (Contrary to popular gardening lore, it is not possible to propagate tuberous begonia from leaf cuttings.) Once planted, the tuber sends out several shoots. At the base of the shoots are small buds. When the shoots are 3 to 5 inches long, cut them below the buds with a sharp knife, taking a thin section of the "tuber" with the cutting. Remove the basal leaves of the cutting and stick it

When dividing iris and other rhizomes—underground stems that grow horizontally—make sure to cut them in such a way that each new section has at least one bud or growing point.

into a container with rooting medium. To keep the cuttings from wilting, mist them frequently or place the container into a transparent plastic bag. Once the cuttings are well rooted, they can be planted out or transferred into a larger container where they will build up the new tuber.

ROOT TUBERS

Root tubers (tuberous roots) are fleshy roots that produce adventitious buds and roots. Sweet potato (*Ipomoea batatas*) is a classic example. Sweet potato is usually propagated from stem cuttings. Cuttings with at least one node can be taken at any time and rooted in two to three weeks in a container with rooting mix. You can also induce root tubers to sprout by placing them in a container with a well-drained potting mix that is kept moist. When the shoots that emerge from the mix are several inches high, dig out the tuber. Most of the shoots will have developed a root system. Cut the shoots below the root system and plant them out.

Dahlia tubers need special attention. Shoots always arise from buds located between the tuber and the old stem, in an area known as "the crown." With a sharp knife separate the tubers, making sure that each one has a bud, which is essential for the following year's growth. Store the tubers in sawdust or peat moss in a cool, dark place until you plant them. Many gardeners prefer to divide the crown in the spring, right after it has started to sprout.

DESIGNING WITH SUMMER-FLOWERING BULBS

BECKY AND BRENT HEATH

S UMMER-FLOWERING BULBS come into bloom at the same time that many perennials and annuals are at their best, and by adding them to your garden you can multiply the colors, textures, scents, shapes, and contrasts in your palette. When thinking about the best way to incorporate summer-flowering plants into the garden, it's helpful to have guidelines. Many of the following suggestions apply no matter what you're planting—perennials, annuals, shrubs, or bulbs.

LIKE WITH LIKE: Plant sun-loving bulbs together with other plants that need a lot of

Opposite and right: Summer bulbs come into bloom at the same time that many perennials and annuals are at their best. Have fun experimenting with them and increase the colors, textures, shapes, and scents in your garden.

The warm golds of black-eyed susans make a lovely foil for the tall spikes of blazing star, *Liatris spicata*, which grows from corms. Both plants are North American natives that love sun and attract butterflies.

sun, and do the same with shade- and wet-loving bulbs, combining them with plants that have similar light and moisture requirements. Once you've met the plants' basic needs, let your own color and design preferences guide you, and have fun discovering which plants are complementary neighbors. Wherever we combine plants with similar needs in our garden, something new and interesting is developing, blooming, or maturing all the time, and we keep going over to see what's happening. Below you'll find lots of suggestions that will inspire you to fill sunny, shady, and continually moist areas with plenty of summer-blooming bulbs.

THINK BIG: Add woody plants, colorful annuals, and a variety of perennials to your summer bulbs display to make your garden more interesting. Include shrubs and trees to give the garden "backbone," or a good, strong spine. This also adds winter interest, nesting opportunities for birds, and a nice background for the smaller flowering plants when they're in bloom.

CREATE A BACKDROP: If your garden bed is backed by trees, a wall, or a fence and won't be seen from all sides, put the taller plants towards the back, the medium plants in the middle, and the shorter ones in front, so that all of them can contribute to the salad of colors and textures. Planting colorful annuals around the edges of the garden helps to tie all the plant material together and puts "shoes and socks" on the larger perennials and bulbs.

EXPERIMENT: In the real world, plants don't fall tidily into the neat groupings we humans create for them. In our garden, we experiment all the time,

White lilies offset the rosy shades of bee balm. Plant lily bulbs deep enough and you won't have to stake them because they will develop stem roots that will help prop up the plants.

looking for plants' "gray areas"—stretching hardiness zones, planting depths, and growing conditions—and we have been very pleasantly surprised to see how adaptable many plants are!

SUMMER BULBS FOR SUN

Hymenocallis (spider lily) is one of our favorite summer bulbs; you can almost watch it come into bloom, it moves so quickly. It is adaptable, growing well in both sun and boggy areas, and is also pest-resistant. Its daffodil-like flower shape, with a distinct cup and six petals, is comfortingly familiar. And as with daffodils, its taste is repellent to deer. 'Sulphur Queen' is fragrant, especially at night, and therefore perfect for a night-garden, but works well in every setting.

Crocosmias contribute long-lasting warm colors to the garden, as the flowers stick around. Every year our *Crocosmia* clumps get bigger and bigger (they're perennial in Zones 6 to 10), and the flowers get better and better. With their sword-like leaves and long, lean flowers, these plants won't take up a lot of room in your beds. Black-eyed susans, other yellow daisies, and dahlias set off their colors beautifully.

Lilies are classic sun-loving bulbs. Plant them deep; they like to have their roots where it's cool. If you plant lilies deep enough, you won't have to stake them because they will develop stem roots that help prop up the plants. Incorporate lilies into the middle or back of the border. Combine Asiatic lilies with larkspurs, yarrows, *Artemisia*, black-eyed susans, dahlias, roses, daylilies, ornamental

In a sunny spot, tall cannas provide a backdrop for dahlias, purple kale, *Celosia* 'Fireglow', and low-growing *Senecio* 'Silver Dust' for a multistory display of summer color.

grasses, Stokes' asters, *Alstroemeria* or coneflowers. Combine oriental lilies with *Cosmos, Coreopsis, Veronica, Echinops*, coneflowers, *Liatris, Canna, Galtonia, Mirabilis,* or *Lycoris.*

The adaptable *Eucomis* has spectacular, plump, pineapple-shaped flower heads, which continue to look great as they form colorful seedpods, extending the bloom for a long, long time. In addition, eucomises make long-lasting cut flowers and are excellent container plants.

The many hues of *Canna* flowers in shades of cream, yellow, orange, red, and pink will contribute nicely to the color scheme of a garden with at least six hours of sunlight per day. Cannas also come in a range of leaf sizes, shapes, and colors, giving you even more design options. Large varieties grow to between 8 and 10 feet, medium-sized varieties hit 4 to 6 feet, and some small cannas reach a mere 2 feet, meaning they're short enough to be in the front of the garden and ideal for containers.

Dahlias come in myriad colors and shapes, and the more you have in your garden the better. Plant them densely among other plants to give them good support; otherwise, they may flop over. This is also a good reason not to grow taller types along a pathway. Keep cutting the flowers through the season, because the more you cut, the better they'll grow and continue to bloom.

In a sunny spot, combine summer-flowering bulbs with larkspurs, purple basils, some of the new, smaller ornamental sunflowers, painted daisies, bachelor buttons, and sweet williams.

SUMMER BULBS FOR SHADE

Contrary to popular belief, many bulbs thrive in shade. *Achimenes,* a terrific groundcover that comes in blue, pink, pure white, salmon, and a mixture of all colors, blooms throughout the summer as long as you keep it moist. *Bletilla,* an easy shade-tolerant bulb in the orchid family, comes in magenta or white and stands about 12 inches tall. *Caladium* hybrids bring light and color into shady locations with their large, brightly colored leaves. White, green, pink, and red caladiums make excellent companions with hostas, ferns, coleus, impatiens, astilbes, and any other shade-loving groundcovers. *Scadoxus* also performs happily in partial shade, with dramatic masses of tiny bright red florets in softball-sized flowers on 8- to 10-inch stems.

To give your garden a tropical feel, try elephant ears, *Alocasia* or *Colocasia.* With their large, often darkly veined or mottled leaves—upright in *Alocasia* and facing out or down in *Colocasia*—they provide drama and structure. *Sauromatum venosum* is right at home in a shady jungle garden. Its large, 1- to 2-foot finger-like leaves on purple mottled 2- to 3-inch stems will look stunning behind caladiums or in front of colocasias and hedychiums.

Sun-loving plants with great foliage will produce fewer blooms in the shade, but their foliage alone can add a lot of interest. *Canna* 'Striata' ('Pretoria') grows best in full sun and may not bloom as well in partial shade; but who cares about those orange blossoms when you can have the terrific yellow and green striped foliage in the shade garden!

A good combination to light up shady corners: ostrich fern (*Matteuccia struthiopteris*), *Hosta sieboldiana*, and pineapple lily (*Eucomis*).

If you live in a climate with really hot midday sun in the summer, partial shade for some of the "full sun" plants might be in order, possibly expanding the list of bulbs that work in the shade.

BULBS FOR BOGGY AREAS

As a general rule, bulbs hate wet feet and need good drainage, but there are exceptions. *Canna, Crinum, Eucomis, Colocasia, Alocasia,* and *Zephyranthes* perform nicely in both flower borders and boggy areas. And there are other bulbs, mostly from warm tropical regions, that feel at home in swampy spots.

Eucharis, with its spectacular fragrant white flowers and deep green leaves, *Hedychium*, with 6- to 12-inch flower heads reminiscent of the wings of tropical birds, and *Schizostylis,* with bright fall-blooming flowers and iris-like leaves, all thrive happily in soggy conditions. *Canna* will also do well in a bog garden.

Achimenes is happy growing in pots and in the flower border but is especially lovely and functional around the ankles of the taller plants in the bog garden and in the front row of the tropical chorus.

Elephant ears enjoy heavy, wet soil. Both *Alocasia* and *Colocasia* produce

gigantic leaves. This foliage provides a strong structural backdrop for other plants in the bog garden. Elephant ears not only thrive in wet

Colocasia (known commonly as elephant ears), caladiums, and coleus give your garden a tropical feel.

soil, but often their hardiness increases by several zones when they are planted in a wet microclimate.

Caladium is one of the best performers to add "shoes and socks" and additional color in the foreground of a tropical-inspired garden. Caladiums come in an array of colors, shapes, and sizes and can be planted in mixtures or by color, depending on your design preference.

Crinum has very large bulbs and produces sword-shaped leaves and large clusters of fragrant, trumpet-shaped white, pink, or wine-red flowers. This pest-proof plant appears to be happy no matter where it's planted. Its flowers seem to last forever and provide us with color throughout the summer. *Sauromatum venosum* also performs splendidly in wet soil, adding another dimension of form with its large, tropical, hand-like leaves.

The dusky lavender to rose flowers of Joe Pye weed, and the yellow and orange blossoms of touch-me-not or jewelweed (*Impatiens capensis*) sway in the breeze in the late summer garden. Cardinal flower (*Lobelia cardinalis*), with its vivid red spikes of fire, contrasts nicely with Japanese iris (*Iris ensata*). And finally, don't forget to include shrubs and trees like swamp magnolia (*Magnolia virginiana*), river birch (*Betula nigra* 'Heritage'), and sweetspire (*Itea virginica*) to give your bog garden "backbone."

Some of the bulbs and plants described here may not be winter-hardy in Zone 6 or colder areas, but because they perform virtually all summer, they are well worth the price and effort to plant. They can be dug up after the first frost nips the aboveground foliage and stored over the winter, or they can be treated as annuals.

Like other elephant ears, *Colocasia* 'Black Magic' is versatile, thriving with its roots in water.

NATURALIZING SUMMER-BLOOMING BULBS

BECKY AND BRENT HEATH

Depending on the climate in your area, certain summer-blooming bulbs will easily become established in your garden. Some will become perennials and come back year after year; others may even naturalize and spread by themselves, without any help from you. The chart below is organized according to climate zones in North America. Plants mentioned in the "Encyclopedia of Summer-blooming Bulbs," starting on page 49, are accompanied by a page number. Please refer to page 101 for a map of the USDA Hardiness Zones.

NORTHERN PACIFIC COAST— ZONE 8

BULBS FOR PERENNIALIZING
× *Amarcrinum memoria-corsii*, p. 55
Amaryllis belladonna, p. 55
Bletilla striata, p. 58
Canna 'Striped Beauty'
Colocasia 'Illustris', p. 63
Crinum 'Bradley'
Dahlia 'Park Princess'
Eucomis autumnalis, p. 73
Galtonia candicans, p. 74
Hemerocallis, p. 79
Incarvillea delavayi 'Snowtop'
Lilium, p. 84
Lycoris radiata, p. 86
Nerine bowdenii
Oxalis lasiandra
Schizostylis coccinea, p. 92
Sternbergia lutea, p. 95
Zantedeschia 'Cameo'

BULBS FOR NATURALIZING
Crocosmia masoniorum
Dichelostemma ida-maia, p. 70
Liatris spicata, p. 83
Mirabilis jalapa
Triteleia laxa, p. 97
Zephyranthes candida, p. 99

CENTRAL PACIFIC COAST— ZONES 8 TO 9

BULBS FOR PERENNIALIZING
× *Amarcrinum memoria-corsii*, p. 55
Canna 'Striata' ('Pretoria'), p. 62
Crinum × *powellii*, p. 65
Dahlia 'Orange Nugget'
Eucomis comosa, p. 73
Hedychium 'Kinkaku'
Lilium 'Star Gazer'
Zantedeschia aethiopica 'Green Goddess'

BULBS FOR NATURALIZING
Agapanthus, p. 51
Amaryllis belladonna, p. 55
Babiana
Calochortus luteus 'Golden Orb'
Crocosmia 'Emily McKenzie'
Sparaxis
Tulbaghia violacea, p. 98

ARID WEST— ZONES 5 TO 7

BULBS FOR PERENNIALIZING
Alstroemeria ligtu hybrids
Amaryllis belladonna, p. 55
Convallaria majalis
Crocosmia 'Lucifer', p. 66
Galtonia candicans, p. 74
Hemerocallis, p. 79

Lilium 'Montreux'
Lilium 'Mona Lisa'
Lilium speciosum 'Uchida'
Lycoris squamigera, p. 85
BULBS FOR NATURALIZING
Dichelostemma ida-maia, p. 70
Liatris spicata, p. 83
Mirabilis jalapa
Triteleia laxa, p. 97
Triteleia 'Corrina', p. 97

ROCKY MOUNTAINS—ZONES 2 TO 4
BULBS FOR PERENNIALIZING
Hemerocallis, p. 79
Liatris spicata 'Alba'
Lilium 'Black Beauty', p. 85
Lilium 'Pink Perfection'
Lilium 'Pretender'
Lilium regale 'Album'
Lycoris squamigera, p. 85
Triteleia, p. 97
BULBS FOR NATURALIZING
Dichelostemma ida-maia, p. 70
Liatris spicata, p. 83
Lilium lancifolium
Triteleia laxa, p. 97

CENTRAL REGION AND GREAT PLAINS—ZONES 5 TO 6
BULBS FOR PERENNIALIZING
Convallaria majalis
Dichelostemma ida-maia, p. 70
Galtonia candicans, p. 74
Hemerocallis, p. 79
Lilium 'Nepal'
Lilium speciosum 'Uchida'
Lilium 'Time Out'
Lycoris squamigera, p. 85
Schizostylis, p. 92
Triteleia laxa 'Queen Fabiola', p. 97
BULBS FOR NATURALIZING
Liatris spicata, p. 83
Lilium lancifolium

NORTHERN CENTRAL REGION—ZONES 3 TO 4
BULBS FOR PERENNIALIZING
Hemerocallis, p. 79
Liatris spicata 'Alba'
Lilium 'Brunello'
Lilium 'Grand Cru'
Lilium 'Menton'
Lilium 'Vivaldi'
Lilium regale
Lycoris squamigera, p. 85
BULBS FOR NATURALIZING
Liatris spicata, p. 83
Lilium lancifolium

SOUTHERN CENTRAL REGION—ZONES 7 TO 8
BULBS FOR PERENNIALIZING
Alstroemeria aurea 'Lutea'
Amarcrinum, p. 55
Anemone coronaria
Bletilla striata, p. 58
Canna 'Cleopatra', p. 62
Crinum × *powellii*, p. 65
Eucomis comosa, p. 73
Galtonia candicans, p. 74
Gladiolus, p. 74
Hedychium coronarium, p. 78
Hemerocallis, p. 79
Lycoris radiata, p. 86
Ornithogalum saundersiae, p. 86
Oxalis triangularis spp. *papilionacea*
Schizostylis, p. 92
Sparaxis
Sternbergia lutea, p. 95
Zantedeschia 'Mango'
BULBS FOR NATURALIZING
Crocosmia masoniorum
Dracunculus vulgaris
Habranthus robustus, p. 78
Liatris spicata 'Alba'
Lilium lancifolium
Sauromatum venosum, p. 90
Zephyranthes rosea

GULF COAST— ZONES 8 TO 9

BULBS FOR PERENNIALIZING

× *Amarcrinum memoria-corsii*, p. 55
Bletilla striata, p. 58
Canna 'Omega'
Colocasia esculenta, p. 62
Crinum 'Bradley'
Crocosmia 'Emberglow'
Curcuma alismatifolia
Dahlia 'Bishop of Llandaff'
Dracunculus vulgaris
Eucomis bicolor, p. 73
Galtonia viridiflora
Gladiolus, p. 74
Gloriosa superba 'Rothschildiana'
Hedychium coccineum, p. 79
Hemerocallis, p. 79
Hippeastrum
Incarvillea delavayi
Lilium 'Avignon'
Lycoris radiata, p. 86
Nerine
Ornithogalum saundersiae, p. 86
Oxalis tetraphylla 'Iron Cross'
Polianthes tuberosa 'The Pearl', p. 89
Scadoxus multiflorus
Sprekelia formosissima
Sternbergia lutea, p. 95
Tigridia pavonia 'Aurea', p. 97
Tulbaghia fragrans
Zantedeschia 'Pink Persuasion'

BULBS FOR NATURALIZING

Globba schomburgkii (*G. marantina*) 'Yellow Dancing Lady'
Habranthus robustus, p. 78
Hymenocallis 'Sulphur Queen'
Liatris spicata, p. 83
Mirabilis jalapa
Oxalis tetraphylla 'Iron Cross'
Zephyranthes 'La Buffa Rose', p. 100

GREAT LAKES— ZONES 5 TO 7

BULBS FOR PERENNIALIZING

Convallaria
Dichelostemma ida-maia, p. 70
Galtonia viridiflora
Hemerocallis, p. 79
Liatris spicata, p. 83
Lilium 'Avignon'
Lilium 'Bright Star'
Lilium 'Muscadet'
Lilium pumilum
Lycoris squamigera, p. 85
Schizostylis, p. 92

BULBS FOR NATURALIZING

Convallaria
Liatris spicata, p. 83
Lilium regale

APPALACHIAN REGION— ZONES 5 TO 6

BULBS FOR PERENNIALIZING

Alstroemeria aurea 'Orange King'
Convallaria
Dichelostemma ida-maia, p. 70
Galtonia candicans, p. 74
Hemerocallis 'Stella de Oro'
Liatris spicata 'Alba'
Lilium 'Casa Blanca'
Lycoris squamigera, p. 85
Triteleia laxa 'Queen Fabiola', p. 97

BULBS FOR NATURALIZING

Liatris spicata, p. 83
Lilium pumilum
Mirabilis jalapa

SOUTHERN ATLANTIC COAST— ZONES 8 TO 9

BULBS FOR PERENNIALIZING

× *Amarcrinum memoria-corsii*, p. 55
Bletilla striata, p. 58
Canna 'Wyoming', p. 62
Crinum 'Ellen Bosanquet', p. 65
Crocosmia 'Norwich Canary'
Eucomis bicolor, p. 73

Gladiolus communis
Hedychium gardnerianum, p. 79
Hemerocallis 'Stella de Oro'
Incarvillea 'Snowtop'
Lilium aurantum 'Tom Thumb'
Lycoris radiata, p. 86
Ornithogalum saundersiae, p. 86
Oxalis tetraphylla 'Iron Cross'
Sternbergia lutea, p. 95
Triteleia 'Corrina', p. 97
Zantedeschia albomaculata
BULBS FOR NATURALIZING
Convallaria majalis
Dracunculus vulgaris
Habranthus robustus, p. 78
Liatris spicata, p. 83
Sauromatum venosum, p. 90
Zephyranthes citrina, p. 99

MID-ATLANTIC COAST— ZONES 6 TO 8
BULBS FOR PERENNIALIZING
Alstroemeria ligtu hybrids
× Amarcrinum memoria-corsii, p. 55
Bletilla striata, p. 58
Canna 'Striata' ('Pretoria'), p. 62
Convallaria
Crinum × powellii, p. 65
Crocosmia 'Emily McKenzie', p. 66
Eucomis comosa, p. 73
Gladiolus callianthus, p. 76
Hedychium coronarium, p. 78
Incarvillea delavayi
Lilium 'Casa Blanca'
Lycoris radiata, p. 86
Ornithogalum saundersiae, p. 86
Oxalis regnellii
Sternbergia lutea, p. 95
Zantedeschia aethiopica
Zephyranthes candida, p. 100
BULBS FOR NATURALIZING
Anemone coronaria
Habranthus robustus, p. 78
Liatris spicata, p. 83
Lilium henryi

Lycoris radiata, p. 86
Sauromatum venosum, p. 90

EAST CENTRAL REGION— ZONES 5 TO 7
BULBS FOR PERENNIALIZING
Convallaria
Dichelostemma ida-maia, p. 70
Galtonia candicans, p. 74
Hemerocallis 'Pardon Me'
Liatris spicata, p. 83
Lilium 'Bright Star'
Lilium 'Le Reve'
Lilium 'Shirley'
Lilium speciosum 'Album'
Schizostylis, p. 92
Triteleia, p. 97
BULBS FOR NATURALIZING
Convallaria
Liatris spicata, p. 83
Lilium species, p. 84

NEW ENGLAND— ZONES 3 TO 5
BULBS FOR PERENNIALIZING
Convallaria
Dichelostemma ida-maia, p. 70
Galtonia candicans, p. 74
Hemerocallis 'Happy Returns'
Liatris spicata, p. 83
Lilium 'African Queen'
Lilium 'Black Beauty', p. 85
Lilium 'Grand Cru'
Lilium henryi
Lycoris squamigera, p. 85
Triteleia 'Queen Fabiola', p. 97
BULBS FOR NATURALIZING
Liatris spicata, p. 83
Lilium lancifolium
Mirabilis jalapa

GROWING SUMMER BLOOMERS IN CONTAINERS

TOVAH MARTIN

I N NEW ENGLAND, as in other cool climates, it's easiest to grow summer-flowering bulbs in containers. Although some summer bulbs claim to be marginally hardy in our neck of the woods, it just doesn't seem wise to tempt fate. Not only are winters cold here, but autumns are unpredictable, creeping in with killing frosts when you least expect a cold snap. Those of us who don't keep our ears permanently tuned to the weather forecast find it easier and less stressful to whisk containers indoors when the temperature drops rather than run out with flashlights and shovels, trying to find stubs that are slipping into dormancy as the thermometer plummets.

Those are the practical reasons why I grow summer-flowering bulbs in containers. From a less objective standpoint, I host my eucomises, dahlias, hymenocallises, acidantheras (renamed *Gladiolus callianthus*), and callas in containers because they look lovely on my back porch. I put them in pots so that I can shuffle them around at whim. What's more, I can never remember the exact colors of the dahlias, so I move them into color compositions when they open. And even as it unfolds, *Dahlia* 'Swan's Gold Medal' changes hue daily as its 7-inch-wide blooms unfurl. Part of the fun of gardening is making a moveable feast for the eyes.

FOCAL POINTS IN CONTAINERS

I've dabbled in a few summer-flowering bulbs, but my forays are nothing compared with Becky Heath's, whose entire Gloucester, Virginia, garden is devoted primarily to bulbs, experiments in the field. Ask about her favorites

Opposite: In areas where winters are long and cold and autumns are unpredictable, it's easiest to grow summer-flowering bulbs in containers, making a moveable feast for the eyes that can be rearranged at a whim.

Strategically placed, potted plants like these elephant ears and caladiums hide bald spots that may appear in the garden.

for containers, and she'll immediately rush into long and fervent praise of lilies. "They're tall and regal, like models," she says, "but some people complain that they fall over. Ours never fall, and I realized that we've succeeded where others fail because most people don't plant lilies deep enough." For containers Becky recommends burying lily bulbs 8 to 10 inches below the soil surface. Of course, this requires a container that's deep enough to accomplish the feat. When the bulbs are buried properly, the plants make stem roots that serve as anchors, helping the lilies stand tall, no matter how briskly the breezes blow.

Lilies are Becky's favorite summer-flowering bulbs for the center of a container. Both Oriental and Asiatic lilies give a container height and provide a focal point around which smaller plants can play. The beauty of using lilies as the central figure is that their foliage is handsome before and after blooming. In that capacity, belamcandas, eucomises, crocosmias, cannas, ornithogalums, the taller alliums, and *Gladiolus callianthus* serve the same function as lilies—all promise blossoms, but they also boast commanding foliage to ride out the season. And all form the top-note in a mixed container, although they're equally comfortable growing solo. Hymenocallises also make a certain amount of headway, especially when they're blossoming. However, they tend to send up their fragrant, large, spider-like white blooms early in the season before your container is really taking off.

Some bulbs are grown for their summer foliage rather than blossoms, and colocasias fit that category. Valued for their immense, elephant-ear-like, heart-

Lilies add height to the center of a container and provide a focal point around which smaller plants like caladiums can play.

shaped leaves in shining green (*Colocasia esculenta*) or deep purple (*C. esculenta* 'Black Magic'), they rarely blossom. But who needs blooms when you've got 18-inch-wide leaves? Colocasias need a large container to balance out the leaf span and to act as ballast when the plant is in full glory. But there's no reason why you can't combine *Colocasia* with smaller, more diminutive bulbs. *Colocasia* hates to dry out, and the trick is to find a companion that will tolerate the moist conditions that elephant ears require. Caladiums also prefer moist conditions and require partial shade as well and might prove effective partners in a pot, forming a skirt around the colocasia's waist. Hostas, though not summer bulbs, would also tolerate the moisture, as would irises, but I grow my colocasias as a monothematic planter—they certainly hold their own without competition!

Cannas straddle the line between foliage plants and bloomers. Although they slipped from popularity when bedding-plant displays fell from favor, cannas rose again as container plants. With strong, upright stems that send their arrow-shaped leaves pointing straight toward heaven and with colors that range from deep burgundy to red striped with yellow, cannas will get your creative juices going. If all that foliage color isn't enough, cannas crown the affair with large, bright yellow, pumpkin-orange, or fire-engine-red blossoms. Some gardeners find the flowers too gaudy for good taste. For those who are inclined

Be sure to follow planting instructions and install bulbs at the right depth whether you put them in a pot or plant them in the ground.

toward propriety, a quick snip with the pruning shears will speedily remove the offending flower.

Some summer-blooming bulbs that work well as focal points have too much foliage to make them good bedfellows. Calla lilies and crinums fall into the too-plump-to-share category, and dahlias also seem to work best solo. For excitement, and to accentuate the majesty and colors of these beauties, I use glazed pots or ornamental urns. And I group them side by side with other plants like cupheas, coleuses, and fuchsias that make their colors pop.

Dahlias prefer to be planted deep and dislike a very fertile soil. Although they rarely need supplemental watering when planted directly in the ground, they dry out often in a container and require regular soaking to form a continual supply of buds. The Gallery Dahlias—'Art Deco', 'Cezanne', 'Degas', Leonardo', 'Rembrandt', and 'Singer'—were specifically developed for containers, forming compact, well-branched growth that precludes the necessity of staking.

SMALLER BULBS

Becky Heath calls smaller companion plants "shoes and socks plants," because they fill out any container, furnishing a fluff of flowers and foliage around the base of a taller centerpiece. Trailing tuberous begonias can assume the role;

achimenes, incarvilleas, and oxalises also work well in that capacity. In fact, all of the above are primarily grown in pots. Both Becky and I agree that they function best and look particularly handsome when framed in a container.

To accompany larger containers, you might want to cluster a few smaller pots around them. Kaempferias, caladiums, alstroemerias, eucomises, oxalises, the smaller calla lilies, and achimenes make handsome companion plants.

POTTING BULBS

The trick to potting any container—whether it holds bulbs or any other type of plant—is to tamp the soil down to fill air pockets. Jar the container a few times while filling it (pick it up and knock it lightly on the ground a few times) to encourage the soil to settle. Moisten the soil before potting to help it firm up in its new home.

Most garden centers sell packaged potting soil specifically formulated for containers. It's easiest to purchase these pre-mixed potting soils, but not all mixes are created equal. Test mixes for suitability by lifting the bag to gauge the weight of the contents. A very lightweight mix probably has a too-generous portion of peat moss and is deficient in loam and compost. Of course, you can always mix in compost purchased separately.

Most bulbs come with planting instructions—follow them, whether you're locating the bulbs in a container or in the ground.

AFTER THE SHOW IS OVER

Container-grown bulbs should be overwintered in a cool, dry, dark area. Even if the bulb is hardy in your region, it's not likely to survive outdoors in a container. In fact, if the container is terra-cotta or cement, it should probably move indoors as well; if it is subjected to a cycle of repeated freezing and thawing, it might crack.

Most bulbs can endure a light frost (check the planting recommendations when the bulbs arrive); however, many begin to look tired before the season winds to a close. To coax dormancy along, withhold water, cut back the foliage to the base, shake off the soil, and let the bulbs dry in the sun for a few hours before bringing them indoors. They'll be ready to plant the following spring when frost is no longer a threat in your area. Or, get a jump on the growing season by starting them indoors in April or May (see "Year-round Care of Summer Bulbs," page 14).

PESTS AND DISEASES OF BULBS

JACKIE FAZIO

WHETHER YOU BUY BULBS at a nursery or garden center, share plants with friends, or browse and buy from garden catalogues, carefully inspect all your bulbs for soft spots, bruises, and the physical presence of pests. When buying through a catalogue, purchase from a reputable source (see "Suppliers," page 102), and examine the bulbs closely upon arrival.

Be sure to select healthy bulbs whose growing requirements match the cultural conditions in your garden. Plant them at the right depth in a spot with the right light conditions and adequate soil and drainage. Proper culture produces healthier plants and healthier plants are more likely to survive a pest infestation or disease.

Insects and diseases are as much a part of the environment as the plants we grow. Base your decision to treat a problem, whatever it is, on whether or not the pest or disease is a threat to the plant's survival—or to its flower buds, if flowering is an important factor for you that year. Develop a threshold of tolerance for diseases and pests, in particular insects. A plant with a few aphids is not necessarily in danger. In fact, pests like aphids might actually draw beneficial insects such as ladybug larvae, which feed on them, thereby creating a natural balance.

Time has proven that many chemical controls cause far more harm than good in the long term. Pesticides destroy beneficial predators, contaminate soils, and endanger the public's health. What's more, pests eventually become resistant to them. Do not rely on hazardous chemicals to solve pest problems. Instead, arm yourself with some basic knowledge about bulb pests, and you will save both time and money.

Learn about the life cycles of the insect pests that appear in your garden. Find out at what stage in its life cycle an insect pest is most harmful to your plants, at what stage it can be most effectively treated, and if there are predators you can introduce to control it. If a pesticide is the most effective treatment, choose the least-toxic product available. For example, black vine weevils cause the most severe bulb damage as grubs, when they are also the most effectively controlled. So, the best time for treatment is spring, when the grubs are most active.

Learn about the life cycles of diseases and the best times to treat them. A disease must have the proper host plant and the right environmental conditions to thrive. Find out what environmental conditions a disease favors and eliminate them, if possible. Combined with good sanitation, this may be enough to keep diseases at bay. *Botrytis*, a fungal disease, needs cool, moist conditions to spread. So avoid

Ladybug larvae keep aphids, which feed on new leaves and flower buds, in check.

overhead watering and misting of plants to prevent the disease from getting a foothold in your garden and carefully remove blighted flowers, leaves, or entire plants if necessary. And remember never to dispose of diseased or pest-infested plant material in the compost pile. If you choose to use a pesticide to control a disease or pest, read the product label. Be sure to use the recommended dose and apply it only on insects and plants specified on the label.

SQUIRRELS, VOLES, AND OTHER RODENTS

In my experience, the only effective way to keep bulb-eating animals from digging up bulbs is to put a physical barrier around the plants. Chicken wire is pliable and works very well. Plastic netting, usually sold to keep birds off fruit shrubs, is also effective. After you plant the bulbs, place wire or netting on top of the soil, securing the edges to the ground. Remove the wire or netting as soon as the foliage starts to break through the soil surface. An alternative is pepper spray, which is effective, but dissipates with moisture and must be reapplied often.

INSECT PESTS

APHIDS

Aphids are soft-bodied, yellow, red, black, or, most commonly, green insects, which feed on the young tissue of new leaves and flower buds. Symptoms include yellowing leaves, flower distortion, and general loss of vigor. And as aphids pierce and suck, they can also infect plants with viruses. You may also see ants, which feed on the "honeydew" secreted by aphids. Controls include predators such as ladybug larvae (*Hippodamia convergens*) and aphid lion or lacewing (*Chrysoperla carnea*), and least-toxic sprays like insecticidal soaps and horticultural oils.

BLACK VINE WEEVIL

The black vine weevil is a double threat, feeding on plants in both its adult and larval stages. The adult, black with a long snout, hides in dead foliage and leaf litter during the day and feeds at night, leaving behind semicircular notches along the leaf edges. To control the adult weevil, it's important to remove dead foliage during spring and summer, thereby eliminating its hiding places. The half-inch-long, cream-colored larva has a prominent brown head. It is a silent killer, attacking bulbs underground and causing wilting and loss of vigor. Beneficial nematodes (*Steinernema carpocapsae*) are effective in controlling the larvae.

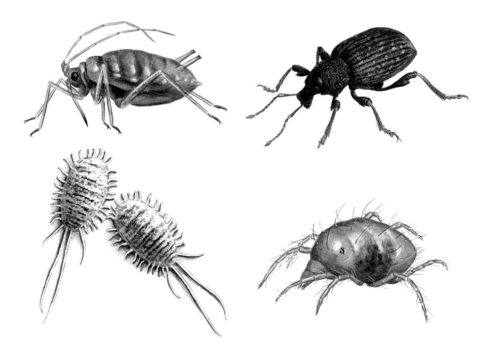

Clockwise from top left: Aphid, weevil, mite, and mealybugs are common bulb pests.

MEALYBUG

Mealybugs are small, white, cottony insects that generally migrate to the crevices of plants, nestling at the bases of leaves and flower stalks. Symptoms include yellowing and distortion of leaves. Controls include a predator called the mealybug destroyer (*Cryptolaemus montrouzieri*). Insecticidal soaps and horticultural oils are the least-toxic chemical controls that work best.

MITES

If you look long and hard, you will learn to recognize the tiny speck-like bodies of mites scurrying across infested leaf surfaces. Most mites feed on the foliage of many different hosts, but a bulb mite attacks genera such as *Narcissus, Gladiolus,* and *Lilium.* Mites are most prolific in warm, sheltered conditions; they cause leaves to become mottled and, during heavy infestations, produce a fine webbing. Predators, most commonly *Phytoseiulus persimilis*, which can be used indoors as well as outdoors, and *Galendromus occidentalis*, which is more adapted to outdoor use, are the most effective control. You should also spray the foliage with water to knock mites off the plant, but be careful not to make the soil soggy, as this may cause other problems.

Top to bottom: Adult lacewing and larva, mealybug destroyer, and ladybug are predators that help control insect pests.

NARCISSUS FLY

The narcissus fly is a small, seldom-noticed insect that is most active in late spring and summer, attacking not only daffodils, but lycorises, galanthuses, amaryllises, and hyacinths, among others. Adults lay eggs at the base or neck of a bulb. When they hatch, larvae burrow to the center of the bulb and hollow it out. Infected bulbs will contain either one large grub (the large narcissus fly) or many small grubs (the lesser narcissus fly). To control the grubs, rake the soil over the crown of the plant once its foliage has died down, to make it more difficult for the grubs to get to the bulbs. Destroy infected bulbs.

NEMATODES

Tiny wormlike creatures, nematodes are normally found in soil and help with the decomposition of organic matter. Most are beneficial, but certain ones do feed on bulbs, causing them to turn soft and blackish brown. Above-ground symptoms include distortion or mottling of leaves. Bulbs infested with nematodes should be destroyed.

SLUGS AND SNAILS

Slugs and snails are both brown, but snails have shells and are rather compact, whereas slugs tend to be longer and can grow quite large. Both have rasping mouth parts that cause streaking on leaf surfaces. They leave behind slimy, iridescent trails, and, in abundance, slugs and snails can decimate plants. To keep their numbers down, eliminate the damp dark spaces they prefer. Sprinkle rough material like gravel or diatomaceous earth around plants as a deterrent, as slugs and snails are very sensitive to rough surfaces.

THRIPS

Thrips are tiny insects that hide in the folds and crevices of leaves and flower buds, where they feed with a rasping-sucking action. Symptoms include brown or silver streaking on leaves and flowers and flower distortion. Thrips can transmit viral diseases as they feed. Since they are mostly hidden, thrips are difficult to reach with insecticidal sprays; use an insecticide that leaves behind a residue and will be ingested by the insects after spraying. You can also try a predatory mite (*Neoseiulus cucumeris*) that feeds on young thrips.

DISEASES OF BULBS

BOTRYTIS

A fungal disease that favors cool, damp conditions, *Botrytis* can infect both bulbs and leaves. It starts as tiny yellow to orange-brown spots on both leaves and bulbs and can advance to a gray mold covering leaf surfaces and bulbs. To control the spread of *Botrytis*, space plants far enough apart to allow for good air cir-

Left: Some microscopic nematodes are harmful.
Right: Slugs and snails can decimate the foliage of bulb plants in moist areas.

culation, water in the morning, keeping foliage and flowers dry, and avoid planting in deeply shaded areas. Destroy any bulbs affected by the disease.

DAMPING-OFF

Caused by various soilborne fungi, damping-off is mostly a problem with seedlings. It attacks plants at the soil line: The stems turn black as the tissue dies and the plants collapse. Good air circulation and well-drained soil can help keep damping-off at bay.

MILDEWS

There are two kinds of mildews, downy and powdery, both caused by fungi. Downy mildew likes low temperatures and high humidity and develops on the undersides of infected leaves as soft, downy growths. Powdery mildew is most apparent in late summer, as it favors

The streaks on the gladiolus are a sign that thrips, tiny insects, were feeding on the flower buds.

warmer weather. The disease spreads as fungal spores are carried from plant to plant by the wind. The fungus itself appears on the undersides of older leaves as a whitish gray web-like substance that spreads to the entire leaf, which will eventually turn yellow and fall off. One application of horticultural oil in early summer prevents many spores from germinating and keeps both diseases to a minimum. Pick a cool day to apply the oil.

VIRUSES

Insects like aphids and thrips are primarily responsible for spreading viruses. As they feed, these insects transmit any viruses they may carry to the plants they visit. Symptoms of viral infection include yellow streaking of foliage, distortion and streaking of flowers, and overall weakening of the plants, which results in a lack of bloom and eventual death. Viral diseases cannot be controlled once plants are infected. Prevent viral infections by controlling the insects that carry and transmit them. To limit the spread of viruses, use good sanitation: Dip your tools in alcohol between cuts or use disposable razor blades for trimming.

ENCYCLOPEDIA OF SUMMER-BLOOMING BULBS

C. COLSTON BURRELL, SCOTT CANNING, NANCY GOODWIN, CHUCK LEVINE

THE GROUP OF SUMMER BULBS described on the following pages is by no means exhaustive, but it includes the plants the contributors most admire and find most useful in their work as gardeners. Many of the plants discussed come from warm-temperate and tropical areas and may not be hardy in the colder regions of North America. Please refer to the chapters "Year-round Care of Summer Bulbs," page 14, and "Growing Summer Bloomers in Containers," page 36, for additional information on growing bulbs not hardy in your area.

Opposite: summer-blooming *Allium moly*.

Achimenes species
MAGIC PLANT, PANSY VIOLET

The flat, perky faces of pansy violets belie their kinship to the familiar African violet (*Saintpaulia*). They are more reminiscent of pansies, though the flowers lack the central flare common in violas. Plants have fleshy, jointed tubers and produce multiple leafy stems with dozens of axillary (between stem and branch) flowers. The quilted, rich green leaves are borne in pairs up the stems, which continue to elongate and flower throughout the summer growing season.

NATIVE HABITAT Tropical America
HARDINESS ZONES 7 (with winter protection) to 11
HOW TO GROW *Achimenes* is absolutely indestructible. The odd dry tubers, which resemble stiff catkins, give rise to a wealth of flowers, hence the common name magic plant. Plant tubers in spring in light but rich soil in a lightly to partially shaded garden bed and, in areas where they are hardy, leave them in the ground over the winter. If you grow them in containers, add a sprinkling of Osmocote to the potting mix, as plants bloom best when they're fertilized well. New shoots emerge like the anemic eyes on a forgotten potato, but rich green leaves soon expand, followed by the showy flowers. Plants thrive in heat and will not begin growing until temperatures warm up in spring. When watering take care to keep the foliage dry, as cold water will cause brown spots on the leaves. If

Achimenes produces a wealth of flowers throughout the summer growing season, hence the common name magic plant.

Agapanthuses are tough plants that look good even if they aren't in bloom. Left to grow undisturbed, they form vigorous clumps.

you're growing them in pots, begin withholding water in autumn and allow the foliage to dry off. You can store the tubers in the pot, or knock them out and store them in dry peat moss in a cool, dry place. Repot in fresh soil in the spring.

CULTIVARS AND RELATED SPECIES 'Blue Sparks' has lovely blue-violet flowers; 'Harry Williams' is bright red; 'Prima Donna' lives up to its name with rose-pink flowers; and 'Snow Princess' is virginal white with a pink eye. All are hardy in Zones 8 to 11.

COMPANION PLANTS Let color be your guide when choosing companions for *Achimenes*. I like the purple ones with orange Mexican flame creeper (*Senecio confusus*, also known as *Pseudogynoxys chenopodioides*) and firecracker plant (*Cuphea*)

for a lively contrast. For a more dreamy effect, use pink-flowered *Achimenes* with licorice plant (*Helichrysum petiolare*), and a purple-leafed coral bell like *Heuchera* 'Velvet Night'. In the ground, pansy violets make a colorful summer groundcover around flowering shrubs; they also combine nicely with ferns and sedges in a partially shaded spot. *—CB*

Agapanthus species
AGAPANTHUS

With about 12 rhizomatous species, agapanthuses are a versatile and rugged bunch, and lately gardeners have become more appreciative of their virtues. Bold clumps of strap-shaped leaves with pendulous tips lend the plant a fountain-like grace. Flower scapes rise well above the foliage. Flower colors range from the deepest purple through sky blue to white; clear blues predominate. **NATIVE HABITAT** Southern Africa **HARDINESS ZONES** 7 to 10 **HOW TO GROW** Agapanthuses prefer moist and well-drained soil in full sun, but are not fussy. Feed them with a balanced granular or liquid fertilizer during active growth, from spring into summer. These plants are largely trouble-free, but watch for slugs and snails. Avoid overwatering in hot, humid weather, as it makes the plants prone to a fungal infection that leads to leaf-tip dieback. *Agapanthus* is best left undisturbed to form vigorous clumps. In fact, it can stand considerable crowding in a container. When dividing becomes necessary, wait till early spring and use a sharp spade or knife. Keep agapanthuses slightly dry in winter. Overwinter containers in a cool frost-free space. Some light is best for evergreen types, but full sun is not necessary for winter storage. Move pots back outside after the danger of frost has passed and top-dress with some fresh soil and granular fertilizer. **CULTIVARS AND RELATED SPECIES** *Agapanthus* fits seamlessly into today's garden designs, which rely on tough plants that have good looks even when they aren't in bloom. Vigorous types such as 'Thunderhead' may reach 6 feet and can shine at the back of the border, while the more demure 'Peter Pan' blooms at 10 to 14 inches and makes for great edging material. These two varieties give an indication of the huge range of sizes, so what you choose depends largely on your size and color preferences. *A. campanulatus* and *A. inapertus* are deciduous and more cold-hardy than the evergreen *A. africanus*. Hybrids derived from them, such as the deciduous Headbourne hybrids are among the most cold-hardy (Zone 7; 6 with protection). In the intermediate range (about 2½ feet), 'Blue Triumphator' and 'Bressingham White' are highly recommended (Zone 7 with protection). The species are not as vigorous as the hybrids and are recommended only for the specialist. Variegated forms exist for the aficionado. **COMPANION PLANTS** Dahlias, heleniums, sunflowers, and goldenrods provide lovely contrasts. Early asters make harmonious companions. —*SC*

Allium species
ORNAMENTAL ONION

Summer-blooming alliums provide a sense of continuity in the garden, taking over from the showy spring-flowering forms when the weather heats up, and continuing until the nights cool down. If Southerners grew all the alliums that survive in their climate, they could have at least one species blooming from late winter through fall. All alliums, flowering onions related to chives and garlic, grow from bulbs, though in some species the bulbs are barely discernible. Most have umbels of small flowers on stalks that rise above the foliage. **NATIVE HABITAT** Most of the 700 species of alliums come from the

Northern Hemisphere. Some are native to dry rocky areas, some to meadows, and others to moist sites. **HARDINESS ZONES** 3 to 10, depending on the species

HOW TO GROW All alliums grow well in full sun with good drainage. Plant in mid-spring through early fall. A light mulch, such as shredded leaves, will protect the tender alliums in areas that are colder than recommended, and will also keep the soil moist, eliminating the need for irrigation. Increase alliums by seed or division.

CULTIVARS AND RELATED SPECIES
A. flavum, the best yellow-flowered species, has gray-blue foliage and umbels of nodding or erect flowers (Zone 5). North American native *A. cernuum* is an elegant plant with nodding umbels of flowers from white through pink (Zone 6). Fragrant, white-flowering *A. tuberosum* makes a fine show in August with full heads of star-like blossoms. The leaves are excellent as a mild substitute for garlic in salads. *A. tuberosum* seeds prolifically but is easily controlled if you cut off the spent flower stalks before the seeds ripen (Zone 3). Diminutive *A. saxatile* blooms for a long time in mid-summer with pink or white flowers and is only about 6 inches high (Zone 3). *A. senescens* blooms all summer long. Heads of blue-violet flowers on 12- to 15-inch stalks above the leafy base provide constant color in full sun. The many forms of this species vary in leaf color—some green, others blue-green (Zone 5). The smallest, *A.*

Most alliums have umbels of small flowers on stalks that rise above the foliage.

senescens subspecies *glaucum,* is fine for a rock garden. The last of the species to bloom just before fall, it has flowers similar to those of its cousins above a base of twisted, gray-blue leaves.

COMPANION PLANTS Grow yellow-flowering *A. flavum* through a base of *Ajuga pyramidalis* 'Metallica Crispa'. Try *A. tuberosum* with *Heuchera* 'Palace Purple' or underneath pink-flowered roses, such as 'Pink Pet'. *A. saxatile* is wonderful in a rock garden or at the edge of a border. *A. senescens* mixes well with kniphofias, daylilies, and *Saponaria* × *lempergii* 'Max Frei'. *A. cernuum* is excellent in an herb garden with oregano or thyme, or as a companion for roses. *—NG*

In the fall, move tropical *Alocasia* indoors, where it will make a lovely houseplant.

Alocasia macrorrhiza
GIANT TARO, ELEPHANT EAR

Lush, heart-shaped leaves point skyward on the thick, succulent leaf stalks of this elegant tropical species that is closely related to *Colocasia*. The huge leaves are carried in dense, multi-stemmed clumps on thick stems that become woody and trunk-like with age. Leaves on mature plants can reach a height of 6 feet or more. This tropical beauty makes a bold and exciting statement in any garden.

NATIVE HABITAT Swamps and low woodlands in tropical and subtropical Asia

HARDINESS ZONES 8 to 11

HOW TO GROW There are a number of alocasias available to adventurous gardeners with a flair for the exotic. The best species for summer bedding are those from subtropical or mountainous regions, where nights are cool. The tropical species are sensitive to cold, beginning growth late in spring and slowing down in fall when nights drop below 50° F. Giant taro has a voracious appetite, so plant it in a container or garden bed in rich, humusy soil laced liberally with Osmocote. During active growth, plants need consistent moisture, and will even thrive in standing water, though it is not requisite. Alocasias are lovely houseplants, so if they aren't hardy in your area you may pot them at the end of the season and keep them actively growing through the winter in a brightly lit spot indoors. Or dig up and dry the tuberous rootstock after the first light frost, shake off excess soil, and store in peat moss in a cool, dry place.

CULTIVARS AND RELATED SPECIES *A.* 'Hilo Beauty' looks more like a *Colocasia*, with out-facing, heart-shaped leaves attractively mottled with creamy yellow (Zones 9 to 11). *A. odora* is a dwarf species, very similar to giant taro in all respects, well suited to containers and small gardens. Plants reach 3 to 4 feet in height, with diminutive leaves a foot or so long (Zones 9 to 11). *A.* 'Portadora' (Zones 8 to 11) has enormous arrow-shaped leaves with wavy margins on short, stout stems. Stunning!

COMPANION PLANTS This commanding plant is always the main event in any container or bed. Some good subordinate players include cannas, especially those with richly colored leaves for contrast, as well as dahlias, coleus, sages, and sunflowers. In light to partial shade, create a lush, tropical look with ferns, Bowle's golden sedge (*Carex alata* 'Aurea'), daylilies, and hostas. —*CB*

× *Amarcrinum memoria-corsii*
AMARCRINUM

This hybrid member of the amaryllis family—an intergeneric cross between two South African bulbs of different genera, *Amaryllis belladonna* and *Crinum moorei*—blooms at the peak of summer's heat. Its amaryllis parent gives the flower an exquisite pink color and form, while the crinum gives the plant hardiness and broad, flat, medium green leaves, evergreen in mild climates. Soft pink, lily-like flowers with white throats shading to green open day after day on stalks that grow to 2 feet. Each stalk may bear 12 or more buds that open to delicately scented flowers. The plants grow from very large bulbs.

NATIVE HABITAT Garden hybrid
HARDINESS ZONES 7 to 10
HOW TO GROW These plants need full sun and heat to bloom well, and will tolerate drought. Ordinary garden soil suits them, but rich humusy soil may produce leaves at the expense of flowers. Mulch them well in winter to be certain they survive unexpectedly low dips in temperature. Clumps of bulbs prefer being

Amarcrinum blooms rise above foliage of elephant ear.

left alone and seldom need dividing.
COMPANION PLANTS Mix with lespedezas, crinums, rain lilies, and hibiscus. Grown near crape myrtles, they provide a leafy base to the trunk. —*NG*

Amaryllis belladonna
BELLADONNA LILY, MAGIC LILY

This amaryllis, the only species in the genus, is one of the treasures of August. In late summer, many fragrant, pink, lily-like flowers open on 2-foot stalks, which appear before the leaves. Strap-like, shiny green leaves grow from late fall through winter and die back in early summer.
NATIVE HABITAT South Africa

Grow belladonna lily as a pot plant, moving it to a prime outdoor spot in August when the flowers develop and keeping it in a cool place indoors during the winter.

HARDINESS ZONES 8 to 10

HOW TO GROW Plants need protection in winter as their foliage grows and heat in the summer when the flowers develop. You will have the best results if you grow *Amaryllis belladonna* as a pot plant, moving it into a cool greenhouse when temperatures drop below 20° F. and watering it as you would other houseplants. Give plants a weak solution of water-soluble fertilizer every second week to build large, flowering-sized bulbs. Withhold water and fertilizer in early summer after the foliage dies back. When the flower stalks emerge in the August heat, move the plant outdoors and water it well by setting the pot in a bucket of water until the soil is completely saturated. Although it is easy to grow amaryllises from seed, you will need patience. They may take 5 or 6 years until they start flowering in colors that range from near white to a deep pink.

COMPANION PLANTS Set a pot of blooming amaryllis bulbs near purple-flowered salvias or near a doorway, where they can enjoy the heat and sun. Or use amaryllis to fill gaps wherever they appear.   —*NG*

Anthericum liliago
ST. BERNARD'S LILY

The erect flower spikes with starry flowers and the strappy foliage of St. Bernard's lily may recall the spider plant that graced your college dorm room. Don't be alarmed; they are related. Plants produce a low, vase-shaped crown of stiff, spear-shaped foliage from fleshy, tuberous-rooted crowns. Multiple flower spikes arise from the center of the clump in mid-summer, and plants stay in bloom for a month or more.

NATIVE HABITAT Open meadows in the mountains of Southern Europe

HARDINESS ZONES 4 to 7

HOW TO GROW These delicate yet showy plants thrive in rich, evenly moist soil in full sun or partial shade. They will tolerate full shade but will flower sparsely. Set out potted plants or dormant rootstock in spring or autumn with the crown just below the surface. Avoid setting crowns too deeply. St. Bernard's lily appreciates consistent moisture, but the fleshy roots impart some drought tolerance. Top-dress annually with compost or well-rotted manure to keep the soil rich and friable. Plants are easy to grow in containers as well.

CULTIVARS AND RELATED SPECIES 'Major', a floriferous selection that grows to 3 feet tall, is the form that's most readily available, though it may not be labeled as such. *A. ramosum,* with upright, gray-green leaves and branched inflorescences to 2 feet, is more heat-tolerant and better for the South (Zones 4 to 8).

COMPANION PLANTS St. Bernard's lilies have an understated beauty and are best placed where they can be appreciated at close range. Use them as accents among low-growing plants like black mondo grass (*Ophiopogon planiscapus* 'Nigrescens'), mountain lady's mantle (*Alchemilla alpina*), and creeping speedwell (*Veronica peduncularis* 'Georgia Blue'). The bright white flowers add light and color to a shad-

Install St. Bernard's lily in a spot where it can be appreciated at close range.

ed garden in summer when few other plants are flowering. Place them near an outdoor seating area used in the evening, when the flowers glow in the faintest light.   —*CB*

Belamcanda chinensis
BLACKBERRY LILY

Blackberry lilies are neither blackberries nor lilies, but iris relatives. In many parts of the South they have naturalized at the edges of woods, where they bloom throughout much of the summer. Each flower lasts only one day and has six orange, purple-spotted petals that open wide. Plants begin to bloom by midsummer and continue into fall with attractive light green

B. flabellata has clear yellow flowers that brighten the garden in late fall. The seed capsules do not look as much like blackberries as those of *B. chinensis.* The plant remains about 12 inches high and the flowers lack spots.

COMPANION PLANTS Belamcandas combine well with late-blooming daylilies, blue salvias, and veronicas. They add color to the base of a shady shrub border and are attractive growing near *Danae racemosa* and hellebores. —*NG*

Bletilla striata
CHINESE GROUND ORCHID

Blackberry lily blooms by midsummer and has attractive seedpods in fall.

seedpods. These split when they are ripe to reveal black, shiny seeds that look like ripe blackberries. Pick the fruit-bearing stalks just as the capsules open and the "blackberries" will remain attractive in dried arrangements all winter. Fans of flat, iris-like foliage precede the flowers and die back in winter. Plants may grow to between 2 and 4 feet tall in a season.

NATIVE HABITAT China
HARDINESS ZONES 5 to 10
HOW TO GROW Belamcandas grow best in full sun or light shade with good drainage. They may be divided or grown from seed, often blooming in the first or second year after sowing. In the garden the seeds germinate readily but not pestily.

This beautiful, ethereal terrestrial orchid is enchanting in both foliage and flower. New leaves emerge in early to mid-spring, wrapped around clusters of flower buds, which open to exquisite miniature magenta corsages on 12-inch stems. The flowers last well when cut, so they can be appreciated in the garden or indoors. Fully expanded, long, strap-shaped pleated leaves resemble exotic palms. Plants grow from swollen, bulb-like rootstocks.

NATIVE HABITAT Woodlands and fields in China, Japan, and Korea
HARDINESS ZONES 6 to 10
HOW TO GROW This orchid is surprisingly easy to grow. Set out potted plants or dry bulbs with the crown up to an inch below the surface of humus-rich, well-drained soil. Give them a spot in full sun or partial shade. Established plants

spread to form broad, multi-flowered clumps that are extremely long-lived. Plants spread outward from the center, and older portions of the clump die out as the clump expands. Lift plants after four to five years and discard the old rootstocks. Replant in fresh soil. Annual top-dressing with compost will keep the plants happy. Chinese ground orchids are easy to grow in a container: In spring when temperatures start to warm up, move the potted orchids into a light, cool place or set them outdoors. Overwinter them in the pot in a cold cellar. Keep the soil moist but not wet during storage, so the bulbs don't shrink.

CULTIVARS AND RELATED SPECIES 'Albo-Striata' is an attractive selec-

tion with leaves that are delicately edged in white. 'Innocence' has lovely pale, creamy flowers flushed with lavender. Both are hardy in Zones 6 to 10. *B. ochracea* is a closely related species with butterscotch-yellow flowers that whirl like butterflies on wiry stems. Plants form delicate clumps of narrow foliage that grow to 18 inches tall (Zones 7 to 10).

COMPANION PLANTS A clump of Chinese ground orchids in full flower surrounded by the lush gold foliage of *Hosta* 'Sum and Substance' is a stunning sight. The magenta flowers combine well with pastel pinks and blues, or with bright rich yellows and purples. Use the bold foliage to add a tropical touch to a mixed planting of shrubs,

The new leaves of Chinese ground orchid emerge in early to mid-spring, wrapped around clusters of flower buds, which open to miniature magenta corsages.

Heat-loving caladiums are perfect for the shade in hot climates. In the North, they require a sunny spot to give them the warmth they need to grow well.

or as an accent around a garden sculpture. In colder zones, place a container of flowering Chinese ground orchids in a blank spot within a garden bed as an accent. —*CB*

Caladium bicolor
CALADIUM, ANGEL WINGS

Few plants can match the sheer exuberance of caladiums. With the possible exception of cannas, they outshine all other foliage plants with their brilliant mix of party colors. The cheery, out-facing heart-shaped leaves are stupendous, adding a festive, tropical touch to any garden.

NATIVE HABITAT Tropical forests of the New World

HARDINESS ZONES 10 to 11

HOW TO GROW The one overriding requirement for growing caladiums is heat. They languish in cool temperatures and never kick into full gear until the days get hot and the nights are warm. They are perfect for the South and other hot spots. Plant the dormant tubers outdoors after the last frost date, when the soil warms to 60° F., or start them indoors in moist peat moss in a bright, sunny window. Plants need rich, evenly moist soil and thrive equally well in sun or shade. In the North, a sunny spot is needed to give them the heat they require for best growth. In autumn, lift the tubers immediately after the first light frost. Tubers left in the cold ground will quickly rot. Store them dry in a net bag in a cool place.

CULTIVARS AND RELATED SPECIES 'Aaron' is great for a shady spot, where the white-centered leaves add a spot of light. 'Candidum' is a classic, with white leaves veined in green. 'Gingerland' is a slightly smaller cultivar with leaves that are splotched in white and red. The Florida Series is a group of sun-tolerant hybrids in various shades of red and rose. 'Rosebud' has a starburst of rose-pink on a green background. All are hardy in Zones 10 and 11.

COMPANION PLANTS Caladiums add panache to any planting. White and pale pink cultivars add summer color to a shaded garden planted with hostas, ferns, groundcovers, and impatiens. In a sunny border, combine caladiums with other tropicals like cannas, coleus, and dahlias for a sizzling display. Use them to add height to containers, surrounded by billowing plants like helichrysums and dahlberg daisies to contrast with their bold foliage.   —*CB*

Canna × generalis
GARDEN CANNA, CANNA LILY

Cannas are the bold tropicals people love to hate. Like dahlias, they have drifted in and out of favor with gardeners since they were *de rigueur* in Victorian bedding schemes. Today's cannas combine colorful mop-head flowers with intricately striped or boldly solid foliage in a rainbow of colors. Leaves vary in shape from narrow lances to broad paddles. Plants grow from thick, water-storing rhizomes that form broad, multi-stemmed clumps. Named selections

Cannas vary in height from less than 3 feet, as 'Cleopatra' above, to 10 feet.

vary in height from dwarfs that are less than 3 feet to towering beauties 6 to 10 feet tall. Plants are easily grown as annuals in areas where they are not hardy.

NATIVE HABITAT Swamps and wet woodlands of New World and Old World tropics

HARDINESS ZONES 7 (with winter protection) to 11

HOW TO GROW Cannas are heavy feeders. Plant them in moist to wet, rich soil and they will flower all season long. Set out the rhizomes in soil enriched with compost or well-rotted manure after the danger of frost has passed. Watch out for Japanese beetles, which love cannas, munching the foliage from the tip down. Pick them off and drop them into a container of soapy water. If plants remain in the ground through the winter, top-dress the clumps in spring with manure to satisfy the greedy roots. Most hybrid selections are hardy to Zone 7, provided they get extra protection in particularly cold winters. In colder zones, treat cannas as annuals, or lift the rhizomes after light frost and store them over the winter for replanting in the spring: Cut the foliage back to a foot above the rhizomes and tuck them into moist peat moss in a cool place. If kept too dry they will shrivel, but if they stay too wet they may rot.

CULTIVARS AND RELATED SPECIES
There are dozens of great cultivars. For flowers, try apricot-colored 'Panache', blinding, deep red 'Brandywine', or the popular scarlet 'President'. 'Striata' ('Pretoria', 'Bengal Tiger') combines yellow-striped leaves and orange flowers, while 'Phaison' (Tropicana) has multi-colored yellow- and pink-striped leaves and orange flowers. For purple leaves try 'Wyoming' or the new 'Australia'. The dwarf 'Cleopatra' has intriguing half-maroon and half-green leaves. All are reliably hardy from Zones 8 to 11. You may want to try them in Zone 7. *C. glauca* is a delicate species commonly planted in water gardens. Long, lance-shaped, gray-green leaves stand erect below modest mops of clear yellow flowers in summer and autumn (Zones 9 to 11). *C. iridiflora* has unique iridescent, nodding, carmine flowers. The stout stems of this hard-to-find species are clothed in wide, sea-

green leaves. Fast-spreading rhizomes quickly form dense, tangled clumps (Zones 8 to 11).

COMPANION PLANTS Choose cannas to jazz up either formal or informal borders, as well as bog and water gardens. To enhance the drama of cannas in a mixed border, combine them with the finer textures of sages, goldenrods, and lespedezas for contrast. Canna foliage catches the light like a stained-glass window. For an exhilarating tropical border, choose coleus, dahlias, caladiums, elephant ears (*Colocasia*), bananas (*Musa*), and other bold, colorful plants. —*CB*

Colocasia esculenta
ELEPHANT EAR, TARO

The outrageous tropical elephant ears have been alternately embraced and eschewed by gardeners for more than a century. Today a wealth of selections, species, and hybrids is available, with heart- to arrow-shaped leaves that may stretch to 4 feet long or more. Plants grow from enormous edible tubers, which are used to make *poi* in Hawaii and, more recently, have gained popularity as deep-fried chips.

NATIVE HABITAT Old World tropics
HARDINESS ZONES 7 (with protection) to 11
HOW TO GROW Elephant ears are easier to grow than petunias. Give them rich, moist soil and full sun to partial shade. They also thrive in wet soil, with their roots submerged in a pond or water garden. Planted in ample-sized pots and provided with adequate light and high humidity, all

Tropical colocasias are easy to grow, thriving in rich, moist soil in sun to partial shade. In colder areas, move them inside for the winter or store the tubers in dry peat moss.

species will do well indoors in the winter. You can also store the tubers over the winter in dry peat moss.

CULTIVARS AND RELATED SPECIES 'Black Magic' has delicious plum-purple leaves and petioles (leaf stalks). 'Burgundy Stem', called the violet-stemmed taro, presents its flat-faced, 3-foot, purple-tinged leaves on smoky purple stems up to 6 feet tall. The diminutive 'Red Eye' is a rapid spreader that forms extensive clumps of 1-foot seagreen leaves, which dance in the wind on delicate petioles. Glossy, black-green leaves with 6-foot squid-ink petioles set black-stemmed elephant ear, *C. fontanesii*, apart from other species. This dramatic plant has sharp, arrowhead-shaped leaves up to 3 feet long. Clumps increase rapidly from creeping, black stolons to form stunning clumps (Zones 7b to 11). Black-leaf taro, *C. esculenta* 'Illustris', formerly known as *C. antiquorum* 'Illustris', is dramatically infused with ink-black splotches between deep green veins. This popular ear is well suited to pot culture. In the ground, it romps about from creeping rhizomes. Foliage color holds best when plants are grown in full sun (Zones 7 to 11).

COMPANION PLANTS Elephant ears demand your attention. Combine the huge leaves with smaller plants that will not compete for admiration. Use them in mass plantings with tender perennials and ornamental grasses. Good companions include ferns, bamboos, and sedges. They add a tropical touch along with dahlias, coleus, and other colorful annuals. Or place them in a tub and use them as specimens in the water garden.   —*CB*

Crinum species
CRINUM LILY

Crinum lilies almost make the heat of summer a pleasure. Most open in the evening at the height of the hottest, most humid part of the season, providing gardeners with delightfully scented fresh flowers. Crinum lilies grow from very large bulbs, producing rosettes of broad linear leaves. Flower stalks up to 3 feet high bear many buds that open in succession over long periods. The flowers in shades of green, white, pink, or near purple look like giant lilies. Some droop gracefully and others are more upright. Large, pale green seedpods follow the fertilized flowers.

NATIVE HABITAT South Africa, Asia, South America

HARDINESS ZONES 7 (with winter protection) to 10

HOW TO GROW Crinum lilies grow well in sun or light shade, forming large clumps of deeply rooted plants that are best protected in winter with a deep mulch of shredded leaves. In the wild, they frequently grow in wet sites, but even though they are said to prefer moist soil, they tolerate drought well, blooming after prolonged dry spells. They require a lot of space and may be divided with difficulty, as the large bulbs form a very tight clump.

CULTIVARS AND RELATED SPECIES The "milk and wine lily," *C.* ×

Delightfully scented crinum lilies, like the cultivar 'Ellen Bosanquet', open in the evening at the height of the hottest, most humid part of the summer season.

herberti, with wine-red stripes on a white base, is often found in old gardens in the South; it is one of the hardiest forms. *C.* × *powellii* 'Album' produces tall stalks with pure white flowers over a long period in mid-summer. The pink 'Cecil Houdyshel' blooms almost all summer long, sending up stalk after stalk bearing many buds. 'Ellen Bosanquet' is the most intense wine-red form readily available. It is vigorous in every way, producing large rosettes of shiny green leaves and burgundy flowers from June to early fall. All are hardy from Zones 7 to 10.

COMPANION PLANTS Crinum lilies combine well with summer-flowering shrubs such as lespedezas, vitex, and crape myrtle. The broad leaves form an attractive base for woody plants. *—NG*

Crocosmia species
GARDEN MONTBRETIA

The name *Crocosmia* comes from the Greek *krokos*, saffron, and *osme*, smell, referring to the strong smell of saffron released from the dried flowers when they are steeped in hot water. The brightly colored flowers, held well above the foliage for several weeks from midsummer to fall, are the main virtue of crocosmias. The flower stems may be branched, increasing the impact of the orange-yellow to brick-red blooms, which seem to float above the sword-shaped, conspicuously pleated foliage that sheathes the lower flower stem.

NATIVE HABITAT South Africa
HARDINESS ZONES 6 to 10
HOW TO GROW Plant crocosmias in

Crocosmia 'Lucifer' is one of the hardiest garden montbretias. Planted deeply and well mulched, it can survive winters in Zone 5.

full sun in moisture-retentive soil, but try to avoid spots prone to sogginess in winter. Crocosmias perform better if left undisturbed, so install them in a favorable spot and mulch them well if you're overwintering them outdoors. In colder climates, lift and store corms as you would gladioli. Plants are generally pest- and disease-free. Crocosmia corms multiply rapidly, which is the preferred way to increase the stock.

CULTIVARS AND RELATED SPECIES The popular hybrid 'Lucifer' is reputedly one of the hardiest; planted deeply (10 to 12 inches) and well mulched, it can survive the typical Zone 5 winter. As its name suggests, this 2- to 3-foot-tall cultivar is fiery red. The species *C. aurea* and *C. paniculata* are highly recommended. *C. aurea* blooms at close to 3 feet in bright golden orange, while *C. paniculata* is even taller, with flowers a reddish orange. These species are all on the tender side, hardy to Zones 7 to 8. The hybrid 'Emily McKenzie' is dark orange with red splashes (Zones 6 to 7); 'James Coey', a more uniform dark orange-red (Zone 6, with a little protection). A very popular hybrid is *Crocosmia* × *crocosmiiflora*, known as 'Montbretia' in the nursery trade. It is a 19th-century French cross of *C. aurea* and *C. pottsii*, which has escaped cultivation in many parts of the world and should therefore be avoided in mild climates.

COMPANION PLANTS The warm colors of crocosmias arrive from midsummer into early fall and harmonize with heleniums and goldenrods. They associate beautifully with silver foliage, and the blue and purple salvias. —*SC*

Cyclamen purpurascens

CYCLAMEN

In much of the Southeast and the mild Pacific Northwest, gardeners can have at least one cyclamen species in bloom in the garden every day of the year. Summer-flowering *Cyclamen purpurascens* provides flowers from May until early winter. The exquisitely fragrant flowers have flung-back petals in shades of wine-red to white. The pink and burgundy forms have a darker ring around the relatively wide mouth of the scented flowers. Rounded leaves vary in their degree of lighter, silver-green patterning.

NATIVE HABITAT Europe
HARDINESS ZONES 5 to 9
HOW TO GROW Leaves and flower stalks grow from round tubers, which need some moisture in summer. They don't want regular irrigation, as too much water will quickly kill them. Nor does this cyclamen like being transplanted, so choose your site carefully before planting. When happy, though, it will self-sow, often coming up a considerable distance from the parent plant, thanks to ants, which carry the seeds away as quickly as they ripen—a year after they have set, just as new flowers appear. Gardeners can grow these plants from seeds, too: Start with freshly ripened seeds, capturing them from the opened capsules before the ants find them. Once

South African native Scarborough lilies are most often grown as specimen plants in containers. Their bright red works best as an accent among other colors.

planted, seeds require a warm period (summer), then cold (the following winter), and will germinate during the second summer when the temperature rises. This almost evergreen species comes into flower before the previous year's leaves have faded.

CULTIVARS AND RELATED SPECIES
Among several recognized forms is *C. purpurascens* from Slovakia, which is reportedly easier to grow and more floriferous than the typical form; it often has solid green leaves. The Limone or Lake Bled forms are either silver with a slender green margin or green with beautiful patterns of silver and sometimes purple edges. These require shade and good drainage. *C. hederifolium* often sends up a few flowers in summer but is best con-

sidered a fall-flowering species. All are hardy in Zones 4 (with protection) to 9.

COMPANION PLANTS *C. purpurascens* is beautiful growing above a base of purple-leafed *Viola riviniana* (*V. labradorica*). It likes the same conditions as *Hosta venusta* and ferns.

—*NG*

Cyrtanthus elatus
(Vallota speciosa)
SCARBOROUGH LILY

This plant's brilliant scarlet, open-faced flowers are quite unlike the down-turned tubular flowers of most *Cyrtanthus* species. The Scarborough lily is a showstopper in bloom, reminiscent of an amaryllis, to which it is related, but much more refined in color and carriage. Thick, strap-shaped, evergreen leaves add to Scarborough lily's attractive demeanor.

NATIVE HABITAT Moist meadows and streamsides in South Africa

HARDINESS ZONES 8 to 10

HOW TO GROW As with most amaryllis relatives, plant Scarborough lily bulbs shallowly, with their necks just above the soil surface. Where hardy, set bulbs out in spring or in fall, if you can get them. Plant them a little deeper in the garden than you would in a pot. In colder climates, start bulbs indoors in spring, and plant them out after the danger of frost has passed. You can sink the pots in the ground, or tip them out for direct planting. They thrive in moisture-retentive, rich soil in full sun or light shade. Store potted bulbs over the winter on a sunny windowsill, keeping them cool and on the dry side.

CULTIVARS AND RELATED SPECIES 'Alba' is hard to locate, but worth the hunt for its glistening white flowers. *C. mackenii* has showy out-facing to slightly nodding white flowers and long, narrow, grassy leaves. Red-flowered ifafa lily, *C. obrienii*, has grassy, deciduous leaves and down-turned, red-orange tubular flowers in summer. Foliage appears with the leaves and ripens off in autumn. All are hardy in Zones 8 to 10.

COMPANION PLANTS Scarborough lilies are most often grown as specimen plants in containers. Their bright red works best as an accent to catch the eye amongst other colors. Group them with pots filled to overflowing with billowing masses of geraniums, verbenas, and million bells (*Calibrachoa*). In the ground, they rivet the eye when surrounded by contrasting blue asters, catmint, and sages. Add some dark purple foliage like *Ipomoea* 'Black Beauty' or *Colocasia* 'Black Magic' for accent.   —*CB*

Dahlia species
DAHLIA

Dahlias have been a mainstay of the late-season garden for a century and a half. The species hybridize promiscuously, which has led to the startling range of types available today. There are in excess of 20,000 listed cultivars, and dahlia societies around the globe recognize from 10 to 12 groups. Enthusiasm for dahlias peaked in the 1840s with a passion that rivaled the 17th-century "tulip mania." Prolific and with an extended season of bloom, dahlias retain their popularity today. The Pacific Northwest and upper Midwest are currently hotbeds of "dahlia mania." Together with gladioli and lilies, dahlias account for the lion's share of summer bulbs planted by gardeners. Dwarf and seed strain varieties are suitable for edging or container use; the other end of the spectrum includes massive selections with flowers the size of dinner plates on plants towering 6 feet and higher. Every color is available except true blue.

NATIVE HABITAT Mountainous terrain from Mexico to Colombia

HARDINESS ZONES 8 to 10

Dahlia 'Tanjo'. With tens of thousands of introductions and sizes that range from 1 foot tall to 15 feet or more, dahlias are a mainstay of the late-season garden.

HOW TO GROW Dahlias require full sun and rich soil and should be watered freely. They are heavy feeders and need adequate fertilizing for best performance. In areas where they are hardy, it is especially beneficial to incorporate generous amounts of well-composted manure into the soil prior to planting in the autumn. In colder areas, plant dahlias in the spring and lift, dry, and store them in the fall the same way as you would gladioli. Spacing is very cultivar-dependent: Space bedding types inches apart, and border types grown for competition at least 2 feet apart. Stake these "gorillas" at planting time to avoid damaging the fleshy tuberous roots. In addition, if you're growing them for competition or cutting, remove the two ancillary buds below the primary bud to maximize stem length and flower size. Propagate dahlias by division: Each tuberous root can be separated from the clump as long as a piece of stem, preferably with a visible bud, remains attached.

CULTIVARS AND RELATED SPECIES With tens of thousands of introductions and sizes that range from 1-foot-tall window box dwellers to varieties that reach 15 feet or more, it is hard to make specific recommendations. Refer to garden catalogues of specialty dahlia growers to appreciate the range available. Some older varieties with dark bronzy foliage are back in vogue.

COMPANION PLANTS Dahlias have great garden merit, and numerous varieties are invaluable as garden and edging plants, flowering from midsummer into fall. However, the enormous size and flamboyant flowers of some types can make them difficult to integrate into a mixed garden; they may be better grown as specimens or in a cutting garden. —*SC*

Dichelostemma congestum
OOKOW, BLUE DICKS

Blue dicks add motion and interest to dry gardens in late spring and summer. Dense clusters of lavender-blue flowers held on thin, wiry stems sway in the slightest breeze. The discreet basal leaves seem hardly substantial enough to power the growth and bloom of this charming true bulb. Plants thrive in

North American native blue dicks thrive in arid regions.

arid regions with a protracted dry season.

NATIVE HABITAT Chaparral and dry, open woodlands of western North America

HARDINESS ZONES 5 to 8

HOW TO GROW Plants demand good drainage and a summer baking to persist more than a year or two in the humid East and Midwest. They are so enchanting laced through other perennials that you may want to treat them as annuals and order a dozen new bulbs each year. Plant them in average to rich, well-drained soil in full sun or light shade. They are great for a gravel bed that receives little supplemental water in the summer.

CULTIVARS AND RELATED SPECIES 'Pink Diamond' sports silver-dollar-sized clusters of lavender-pink flowers. *D. ida-maia* breaks the mold with deep red, yellow-tipped tubular flowers that look like lipsticks. *D. capitatum* (*D. pulchella*) is scarce in cultivation but occasionally available from bulb specialists. The soft blue flowers with darker veins are inflated like a balloon. All are hardy in Zones 5 to 8.

COMPANION PLANTS The best companions are other plants that thrive on summer dryness. Try mariposa lily (*Calochortus*), lavender, catmint, Jerusalem sage (*Phlomis*), and prickly-pear cactus (*Opuntia*) with a wealth of ornamental grasses to create the effect of the western meadows where these plants grow wild. Use them in containers, where they will pop up like hatpins through familiar annuals. —*CB*

Eremurus species
DESERT CANDLE, FOXTAIL LILY

The common name, foxtail lily, describes the appearance of the inflorescence fairly well: A stately, narrow, feathered taper that commands attention from afar. In their native habitat, eremuruses populate dry, stony, overgrazed hillsides. Ignored by grazers and browsers alike, the foxtails soar above the desolate stubble. Deer-besieged gardeners, take note of this valuable trait!

NATIVE HABITAT Western and Central Asia

HARDINESS ZONES 5 to 7

HOW TO GROW Eremuruses prefer dry, hot sites and sandy or gravelly soil; they are not suitable for frost-free areas (Zone 8 or higher), and are poorly adapted to wet winter weather. The starfish-shaped root complex is extremely fragile, and must be handled and planted with the greatest care, preferably immediately upon delivery. Plant shallowly and cover with 2 or 3 inches of flinty soil. Protect the plants from wind, carefully staking them if necessary. In areas where winters are wet, a deep, dry mulch is advisable; apply 8 to 10 inches of coarsely chopped spruce or fir boughs in December—recycle your seasonal decorations! Under the most favorable circumstances, eremeruses may self-sow, but the most dependable ways to increase stock are buying from catalogues or propagating from seed, which is a slow process.

CULTIVARS AND RELATED SPECIES
The characteristics of the species *E. stenophyllus* (Zones 5 to 7) predominate in garden varieties. It has 3- to 4-foot foxtails that are a clear yellow. Other species contribute pinks and oranges to the palette. The Shelford hybrids are typical, growing to between 4 and 5 feet tall, and blending salmon, orange, pink, or white, all suffused with yellow. 'Isabel' is pale yellow; 'Rosalind' bright pink, and 'Cleopatra' deep orange. All are hardy in Zones 5 to 7.

COMPANION PLANTS If you are looking for a strong vertical accent in the June garden, this is it, with hybrids rising to between 3 and 6 feet. The tallest alliums, with their globular flowers, play against the foxtails mar-

Foxtail lilies prefer dry hot sites, and sandy or gravelly soil.

Often grown indoors, Amazon lily makes a fine garden plant in summer.

velously. Eremuruses bloom in early summer, and if they have a flaw, it is that they must have full sun until they go dormant in high summer, and then you will have to deal with the void they leave in the garden.   —*SC*

Eucharis amazonica
AMAZON LILY, EUCHARIST LILY, MADONNA LILY

This sweet-scented beauty is often grown as a houseplant, but it needn't be confined indoors. Greenish white flowers like paperwhite narcissus on steroids nod in loose clusters of three to five on 12-inch stalks above a neat rosette of waxy, hosta-like leaves. Indoors, flowers open sporad-ically all season. In the ground, expect bloom in late summer. Plants grow from true bulbs with fleshy roots reminiscent of lily-of-the-Nile (*Agapanthus africanus*).

NATIVE HABITAT Moist streamsides in the Andes from Colombia to Peru
HARDINESS ZONES 9 to 11
HOW TO GROW Amazon lilies require humus-rich, consistently moist soil in a light to fully shaded spot. Set plants out after the danger of frost has passed. They quickly form attractive clumps of foliage that make the best show the first season if several plants are placed together. Larger, established clumps can be spaced farther apart. Lift the plants in autumn before the first frost. Try growing them in a con-tainer, which can be placed in the garden for the summer and brought indoors with the return of cold weather. Keep plants on the dry side when they are not in active growth. In Zone 9 and warmer, plants are reliably hardy outdoors.
CULTIVARS AND RELATED SPECIES *E. bouchei*, a closely related species from Panama, offers five to eight smaller flowers clustered atop 1½-foot stems. It is hardy in Zones 9 to 11.
COMPANION PLANTS Set a decorative pot filled to overflowing with Amazon lily into a bed of lush foliage plants, or place it at the end of a path as a focal point. Install plants at the front of a bed, surrounded by a low groundcover of *Laurentia*, *Ajuga* (bugleweed), or *Mazus*. Add height to the display with gingers (*Hedychium*), coleus, elephant ears (*Colocasia*), and ferns.   —*CB*

Eucomis species
PINEAPPLE LILY

The unmistakable attribute of *Eucomis* is its tuft of leaf-like bracts atop the oblong inflorescence, which gives the flowers an uncanny resemblance to a pineapple. The flowers are particularly long-lasting and attractive, even in fruit. The large speckled bulbs produce a rosette of smooth, strap-shaped leaves, which in some varieties have wavy margins, beautiful coloration, or rich markings. With attractive foliage and long-lasting blooms in late summer, these subtle, luscious beauties deserve to be more popular.

NATIVE HABITAT Northeastern South Africa

HARDINESS ZONES 7 to 10

HOW TO GROW Pineapple lilies need protection from frost and trampling feet, so it's best to grow them in a container with rich soil. In this way, you can display them prominently when they're in their glory, and take them indoors to protect them from the cold during their winter dormancy. Plant bulbs shallowly, with their necks at or just above the soil level.

CULTIVARS AND RELATED SPECIES Three species are readily available from specialty bulb nurseries. *E. bicolor* blooms in July/August, is robust at up to 2 feet, and has greenish flowers edged in purple. *E. comosa* is shorter and darker, blooming at roughly the same time. It includes an outstanding variety, *E. c.* 'Sparkling Burgundy', which has rich burgundy foliage and green-

Pineapple lilies produce attractive, long-lasting blooms in late summer.

blushed purple flowers. *E. autumnalis* has flowers of creamy green, and is the shortest and latest of the bunch. Its 1-foot flower stalk is displayed in August/September. Less commonly available and truly outstanding is *E. pole-evansii*. It can reach 3 feet, is shades of green all over, and is the most remarkable "pineapple" of them all.

COMPANION PLANTS *Eucomis* is best container-grown, as described, and works well either as a specimen or with other plants that won't make the greenish flowers "disappear." Consider the white- and green-flowering types of nicotianas or small-flowered companion plants that draw focused attention to the container. *—SC*

Summer hyacinths can add a wonderful sculptural element to a garden spot.

Galtonia candicans
SUMMER HYACINTH

Galtonias look more like yuccas than hyacinths, but have none of the sharp aridity of the former. A 3½-foot stalk raises about 15 drooping, snow-white bell-shaped flowers above a somewhat succulent rosette of leaves. Gazing at the large, snow-drop-like flowers in high summer has a cooling, refreshing effect.

NATIVE HABITAT Northeastern South Africa

HARDINESS ZONES 5 to 10

HOW TO GROW Set galtonias in a sunny spot in fertile, well-drained soil. They resent drought and disturbance while growing. Hardy to 5° F. with perfect drainage, they must be lifted and stored like hybrid gladioli in areas with very cold or wet winters. They perform better if they can be mulched and left undisturbed. This disease- and generally pest-free summer bulb is easy to grow but slugs can ravage the foliage.

CULTIVARS AND RELATED SPECIES *G. candicans* is the only species readily available, and the hardiest. Other species are worth trying, though. Tender *G. viridiflora* is similar but has green lines on the outside of the flowers (Zones 9 to 10).

COMPANION PLANTS Blooming as the flowers of many perennials begin to fade, galtonias lend freshness and strong vertical accent to the late-summer border. *—SC*

Gladiolus hybrids
GRANDIFLORA GLADS

The 'Grandiflora' glads, which include the vast majority of named garden cultivars available today, are very large plants, with abundant showy flowers. They grow stiffly erect and can be very formal, in colors ranging from decorative to "screaming." Their imposing nature leads gardeners to develop strong feelings pro or con, with few falling into the middle ground. The same named variety can strike one gardener as exquisite and another as funereal. These plants provide a very strong vertical component to a planting, and their utility as cut flowers is the stuff of legend. They are tender and should be planted in spring to bloom in mid- to late summer, then lifted in the autumn for

To extend their bloom season, plant corms of tender 'Grandiflora' glads in spring at two-week intervals.

frost-free storage. The other group of glads available today includes the mostly shorter and cold-hardy early bloomers such as the Nanus varieties, les Colvilles, and the Charm series. These retain both a casual appearance and a carefree nature; they need not be lifted where soil temperatures do not drop below the low 20's (roughly Zone 5 with protection and warmer), and if drainage is perfect, even to 15° F.

NATIVE HABITAT Garden hybrids

HARDINESS ZONES Varies depending on cultivars

HOW TO GROW Gladioli require a sunny site with good drainage and protection from wind. Improve heavy soils with finished compost, leaf mold, and sharp sand. At plant-ing time, a light to moderate use of a balanced fertilizer is recommended. Also recommended is a spring application of bone meal. Plant corms of the tender 'Grandiflora' types in spring when the weather has settled somewhat, and keep planting at two-week intervals to extend the bloom season. Place corms 4 to 6 inches deep and at least 6 inches apart. Plants benefit from regular watering and supplemental feeding with a low-nitrogen/high-potassium liquid fertilizer. The hardier types, such as the Charm Series, les Colvilles, and the Nanus Group (and some Eurasian species) bloom in early summer, and the foliage fades six to eight weeks after bloom, when it should be removed at ground level. They are all hardy to Zone 6 or (with careful placement and perfect drainage and mulch) to Zone 5. The Grandifloras remain green until well into the fall; lift them before the first frost. Remove the season's growth close to the crown with a clean sharp tool. Detach cormlets from corms and dry off both in a warm, dry, airy place before storing in a cool, dry environment. Check regularly to discard any corms that may become unsound.

CULTIVARS AND RELATED SPECIES As with dahlias, named varieties number in the thousands. Consider color, height, and degree of "ruffling" or marking of the tepals. For the perennial border, the hardy types are less formal and flamboyant and associate more easily with other perennials; they are also easier to grow.

COMPANION PLANTS At the back of the border, and in the cutting garden, the Grandifloras consort well with the taller dahlias. The hardy types are well suited to the herbaceous border, but they go dormant in high summer, so careful planting with late-emerging perennials like balloon flower (*Platycodon*) or late-flowering daylilies is a good strategy. Or fill the void with late-season annuals that don't require constant moisture (which would be detrimental to dormant corms) such as zinnias or rudbeckias.   —SC

Gladiolus callianthus (*G. murielae, Acidanthera bicolor*)
GLADIOLUS

Fragrance is reason enough to grow this plant. In late August, magnificent, six-petaled white flowers with dark burgundy throats open in the evening, perfuming the garden with their delightful scent. Iris-like leaves grow to about 2 feet long during the summer on 3-foot stalks. This iris relative was once called *Acidanthera bicolor.* The new classification transfers it to the genus *Gladiolus*, where it is a star.

NATIVE HABITAT East Africa
HARDINESS ZONES 7 to 10
HOW TO GROW Plants grow from annual corms, which replace themselves by producing a new one above the old each summer. Plant these in late spring in a sunny, well-drained location. This gladiolus is

The flowers of *Gladiolus callianthus* perfume the evening garden.

Rain lilies, such as *Habranthus robustus* above, flower from early summer until well after frost. Above, they are shown growing through a ruffle of oxalis.

fully hardy from Zone 7 south but won't bloom after the first summer unless you lift and dry off the corms. Store them in a dry place at 50° to 70° F. during winter.

CULTIVARS AND RELATED SPECIES 'Murielae' is taller and larger than the species. Its long stalks are superb for cutting and the flowers are long-lasting.

COMPANION PLANTS Grow this gladiolus in full sun combined with burgundy grasses such as *Pennisetum setaceum* 'Rubrum' or 'Burgundy Giant'. It looks wonderful with *Salvia* 'Purple Majesty' and rudbeckias.   —*NG*

Habranthus species
RAIN LILY

Rain lilies flower from early summer until well after frost. Unlike zephyranthes, the other rain lilies, the flowers of *Habranthus* species are held at an angle to the stem rather than upright. The six stamens (male flower parts) are held at different levels, some higher, some lower. These plants grow from bulbs and produce narrow blade-like leaves.

NATIVE HABITAT Desert to moist areas in South America and the southeastern U.S.

HARDINESS ZONES 7 to 10

HOW TO GROW These grow best in full sun. Increase by division or by sowing seed. For best results, sow freshly ripened seeds in a flat filled with a well-drained medium. Try to keep the seedlings growing throughout winter and the new young plants will bloom the first summer following sowing.

The lemony gardenia-scented flowers of butterfly ginger open a few at a time.

CULTIVARS AND RELATED SPECIES *H. robustus* produces medium pink flowers that shade to near white in the throat. It blooms throughout summer producing scape after scape, each bearing a single flower. *H. brachyandrus* is similar but has a shorter blooming period, waiting until late summer to flower. The carmine pink flowers are larger with dark burgundy throats. *H. tubispathus* and its rose form, *H. t.* var. *roseus*, are relatively small. The species form has yellow flowers with bronze backs that appear in late summer above leafless bulbs. The leaves grow throughout winter. The rose variety has dusky rose blossoms and blooms much earlier than its yellow cousin.

COMPANION PLANTS *H. robustus* looks good with dark purple verbenas. *H. brachyandrus* is beautiful growing up through *Artemisia* 'Powis Castle' or near purple verbenas. Both *H. tubispathus* and *H. t.* var. *roseus* are attractive with *Tradescantia pallida* 'Purple Heart'. All are hardy in Zones 7 to 10. —*NG*

Hedychium coronarium
BUTTERFLY GINGER, GINGER LILY, GARLAND LILY

The scent of butterfly ginger is reminiscent of gardens of the Deep South, where the moist air is perfumed in summer. Stiff, linear leaves to 2 feet long alternate up the stalk like climbing spikes on a telephone pole. The foot-long terminal flower clusters sport 2-inch, snow-white flowers with the texture of powdered snow. The lemony gardenia-scented flowers with rounded petals open a few at a time, so each cluster sweetens the garden for weeks on end. Plants grow from thick, fibrous rhizomes nearly identical to those of the culinary ginger you find at the grocery.

NATIVE HABITAT Swamps and wet meadows of the Old World tropics; naturalized in tropical America

HARDINESS ZONES 8 to 11 (7 with winter protection)

HOW TO GROW Butterfly ginger is a big plant with a big appetite. Give this glutton rich, consistently moist soil and a spot in full sun to partial shade. Work a generous supply of rotted manure or compost into the planting hole, along with a balanced

78

fertilizer, and top-dress annually with manure to keep the plants healthy. Lift the huge rootstocks in autumn and store them in bushel baskets of dry peat in a frost-free place. Plants are easy to grow in containers.

CULTIVARS AND RELATED SPECIES
H. coccineum produces flaming torches of fragrant orange to red flowers that open simultaneously for a dazzling show. 'Disney' has peachy red flowers. 'Flaming Torch' lives up to its name, with slender spikes of burnt orange-red flowers from late summer through frost; 7-foot stems are produced by the ever-expanding clumps of this hardy Himalayan native (Zones 7 to 10). Kahili ginger (*H. gardnerianum*) has smaller flowers on dense 2-foot spikes atop stems towering over 6 feet. A wealth of hybrids claim this species as one parent. Colors of the mildly fragrant flowers range from the soft yellow 'Moy Giant' and orange-eyed 'Daniel Weeks' to deep orange-red 'Elizabeth' (Zones 8 to 10).

COMPANION PLANTS Gingers fit comfortably into almost any garden setting, from formal borders to lavish woodlands. They add tropical elegance among traditional perennials like border phlox (*Phlox paniculata*) and lobelia. Create a lush oasis with crinums, spider lilies (*Hymenocallis*), bamboo, and elephant ears. Contrast the architectural foliage with fine-textured meadow rue (*Thalictrum*), bugbane (*Cimicifuga*), and iris, as well as ferns, sedges, and grasses. For simple drama, try a pot full of ginger as a focal point or accent in a garden bed.   *—CB*

Hemerocallis species
DAYLILY

The daylily has been cultivated for hundreds of years, both for its exquisite flowers and as a food crop. Daylily foliage comes up fairly early and forms a grassy-looking clump. Each flower rises on a scape, of which there may be many, and lasts for just a day—but flowering can continue for weeks. New varieties are available in multitudinous colors, shapes, patterns, and forms.

NATIVE HABITAT Temperate Europe and Asia

HARDINESS ZONES 3 to 10

HOW TO GROW Daylilies enjoy full sun to partial shade and seem to thrive in ordinary garden soil. Some flower colors, such as the violets, show their color best in partial shade. The soil around the plants should be kept moist for the best flowering. Left alone, most plants will form large healthy clumps, and will stay put where you plant them. The common species *H. fulva* spreads, and sends shoots beyond the original parent plant. It can be used for naturalistic landscaping and makes a nice addition to an alternative lawn or meadow, or for holding banks for erosion control.

CULTIVARS AND RELATED SPECIES
There are literally thousands of cultivars to choose from. *H. fulva* 'Kwanso Variegata' has boldly striped green and white foliage and usually fully double, reddish orange flowers. The tiny rock garden variety 'Penny's Worth' grows only 9 inches tall and has multitudes of

miniature yellow blooms. Other varieties are mammoth in stature, with grassy plumes of foliage and scapes reaching up to 4 feet; flower size can be impressive as well. 'Well of Souls' has flowers measuring to 6½ inches. Other recommended varieties include: 'Bela Lugosi', 'Candy Apple', 'Jacob', 'Crystal Blue Persuasion', 'Dracula', 'Rachel My Love', 'Mardi Gras Parade', 'Mauna Loa', 'Navajo Princess', 'Navy Blues', 'Nosferatu', and 'Noah's Ark'. All are hardy in Zones 4 to 10.

COMPANION PLANTS Daylilies are suitable for the mixed border and are often interplanted with daffodils. Other companions include greater masterwort (*Astrantia major*), geraniums, and false sunflower (*Heliopsis*). Annuals such as sweet alyssum and petunias work well in front of daylilies. Interplant daylilies with small shrubs or perennials such as peonies.　　　　　*—CL*

Hippeastrum × *johnsonii*
HARDY AMARYLLIS, ST. JOSEPH'S LILY

The gaudy Christmas amaryllis, with its gawky flower stems topped with four-square, foghorn-shaped flowers is the picture of hybrid perfection in *Amaryllis*. If these overblown hybrids do not appeal to you, try the delicate hardy amaryllis. This subtle beauty can be scarce in catalogues, but it has been passed around southern gardens for generations. Its bright red trumpets sport narrow petals, each blazed with a white streak that gives the flower a starburst pattern. Strap-like, fleshy

Daylilies flower best if the soil around the plants is kept moist. Left alone, most plants will form large healthy clumps. Above is 'Chicago Apache'.

leaves appear in spring, topped by a cluster of four to six flowers in mid-summer. Plants grow from fast-multiplying bulbs to form multi-flowered clumps to 1½ feet tall.

NATIVE HABITAT Garden hybrid

HARDINESS ZONES 8 to 11

HOW TO GROW Set bulbs out in spring or summer with the nose of the bulb protruding from rich, well-drained soil. Plants grow best in full sun to light shade. To propagate, lift bulbs after flowering, tease the clumps of bulbs apart, and replant into enriched soil. To store bulbs over the winter, lift them, shake off excess soil, and let them air dry for several days. Clean off all soil, and store in dry peat moss until the following spring. Plants take well to container culture. Dry the bulbs off in autumn, and replant into fresh soil in spring when the first new leaves appear at the top of the bulbs.

COMPANION PLANTS Hardy amaryllis has a unique character that may be difficult to incorporate artfully into the garden tapestry. Try a combination with bicolor yellow and red *Salvia × jamensis* 'Sierra San Antonio', creamy yellow 'Hoffnung', yarrow, and variegated moon grass (*Molinia caerulea* 'Variegata'). For a red-on-white look, try a clump of amaryllis in the center of a carpeting groundcover like *Mazus reptans* 'Alba' against a backdrop of Mongolian aster (*Asteromoea mongolica*).

CULTIVARS AND RELATED SPECIES *Hippeastrum* 'San Antonio Rose' is another hardy hybrid, noted for its rosy pink flowers. Dwarf Dutch hybrid amaryllis such as 'Scarlet

Hardy amaryllis is a delicate beauty, popular in southern gardens.

Baby' and yellow 'Pamina' can be planted outdoors in summer. —*CB*

Iris
IRIS

The genus *Iris* includes more than 200 species and thousands of cultivars that all share a flower composed of parts in threes—usually three upright petals called "standards," three down-facing sepals called "falls," and three, often ornamental, "style arms." Irises come in amazing combinations of shapes and colors. Most of the summer-blooming types are fairly tall, and all lack the fuzzy area on the falls known as a beard, which is common in the spring-blooming types.

Most summer-blooming irises are fairly tall and lack the fuzzy area on the falls known as a beard. Above is *Iris siberica* 'Velvet Night'.

NATIVE HABITAT North America, Europe, and Asia

HARDINESS ZONES 4 to 10

HOW TO GROW Most beardless irises prefer a moist or even wet situation in half to full sun and will thrive in slightly acid garden soil. Siberian iris species— *I. pseudacorus, I. versicolor, I. virginica,* and *I. setosa*— and cultivars bloom very early in summer. These are followed by species and cultivars in the Spuria and Louisiana sections and, finally, the Japanese irises. Some irises in the Louisiana section may not be hardy in the North, but are the best choices for Zone 10. Many Spuria cultivars prefer a dry summer. All beardless irises benefit from an organic summer mulch.

CULTIVARS AND RELATED SPECIES *I. ensata, I. laevigata, I. foetidissima,* and *I. pseudacorus* as well as some bearded irises possess forms with boldly variegated foliage, usually called by the species name plus 'Variegata'. Some bearded irises have remontant (reblooming) selections that flower in the summer. Reliable even in the North are white 'Immortality' and yellow 'Corn Harvest'. The Siberian iris cultivars have surged in popularity due to their later bloom period, adaptability, and use as a cut flower. The large and exotic Japanese irises produce the most sensational summer flowers; many have veins, splashes, and borders in purples, pinks, and whites. Hybridizing with the beardless types is in its early stages but progressing rapidly. All are hardy in Zones 4 to 10.

COMPANION PLANTS Beardless irises

Blazing stars are native to the prairies and meadows of eastern and central North America. Most prefer rich, evenly moist soil and full sun. Above is *Liatris spicata*.

combine well with other perennials and annuals in a mixed border. Try them with, or followed by, daylilies, delphiniums, and chelone, wherever an upright accent is desired. —*CL*

Liatris spicata
BLAZING STAR, SPIKE GAYFEATHER

The milky violet spikes of blazing stars weave through the summer garden like exclamation points on a spirited page of prose. Tall spikes bearing dozens of small compact heads open from the top down, a characteristic somewhat unique among perennials. Grass-like basal leaves are longer and broader than those that rise up the 2- to 4-foot stems and mingle with the flowers. Excellent cultivars are available in a variety of colors and sizes. Blazing stars are popular cut flowers that grow from fat corms.

NATIVE HABITAT Prairies and meadows of eastern and central North America

HARDINESS ZONES 3 to 8

HOW TO GROW Spike gayfeather is one of the best garden plants in the genus. The leafy stems are stiff and seldom need support. Plant in rich, evenly moist soil in full sun. Give them plenty of room without competition from other plants to keep them vigorous. Clumps seldom need division for cultural reasons but can be propagated by dividing the corms in early fall.

CULTIVARS AND RELATED SPECIES 'August Glory' has blue-violet flowers on 3- to 4-foot stems. 'Callilepis' is 4 feet tall with deep purple flowers. 'Floristan Violet' has rosy purple flowers perfect for cutting. 'Floristan White' has creamy white flowers on 3-foot stems. 'Kobold' is the most popular cultivar, with dense spikes of mauve to violet flowers held on stiff stems only 2 to 2½ feet tall. Button gayfeather (*L. ligulistylis*) differs from the above species in that the 1-inch, button-like heads on short stalks are carried in open rather than dense rattail spikes. Plants grow 2 to 5 feet tall and are magnets for monarchs and other butterflies. They are found in wetter sites than spike gayfeather, so plant in humus-rich, evenly moist soil in full sun (Zones 3 to 8).

COMPANION PLANTS Gayfeathers are lovely additions to formal gardens as well as informal meadow and prairie plantings. Combine them with coneflowers, asters, goldenrods, butterfly weed, and prairie clover (*Dalea*). In borders, employ their vertical form to add interest to mixed perennials like garden phlox, yarrows, wormwoods (*Artemisia* species), and ornamental grasses.   —*CB*

Lilium species
LILY

Members of the genus *Lilium* are the true lilies, hardy plants that possess a true bulb composed of numerous individual scales. The garden types are usually Asiatic, Oriental, Trumpet, or species lilies. Colors range from snow white, peach, velvet red, and brilliant pinks, to oranges and yellows in solid or blended colors.

If you choose lily varieties carefully you can extend the bloom period from late spring to late summer. Above, an eastern tiger swallowtail visits *Lilium speciosum* 'Rubrum'.

NATIVE HABITAT Temperate regions of North America, Eurasia, China

HARDINESS ZONES 4 to 10

HOW TO GROW Lilies thrive in a relatively moist but not wet, humus-rich soil. Lily flowers like to reach up into full sun while the roots want to remain cool. Each bulb produces at least a single stem, encircled by attractive glossy leaves; many will become handsome clumps in just a few years. If you choose varieties carefully, you can extend the bloom period from spring to late summer. Lilies benefit from a thick mulch of shredded leaves or pine needles. Lilies can be planted in containers at any time.

CULTIVARS AND RELATED SPECIES *L.* 'Black Beauty' is a superlative plant with arching stems that carry black-red, tightly recurved flowers on 3- to 5-foot stems into August. *L.* 'Doeskin', an Asiatic, has many Turk's-cap-type, peach-champagne flowers with cinnamon-red anthers on stems 3 to 4 feet tall. It quickly multiplies, forming a healthy colony in just a few years. Other recommended species and cultivars include: 'Anaconda', *L. martagon,* 'Scheherazade', 'Tiger Babies', 'Uchida', 'Viva', and 'White Henryi'. The Turk's-cap, *L. superbum,* is a hardy species native to the U.S. Species lilies are often used in prairie restorations and meadow gardens. All are hardy in Zones 4 to 10.

COMPANION PLANTS Lilies are often planted among groundcovers such as *Lamium maculatum* and low-growing annuals such as sweet alyssum. They combine well in the shrub border, backed by viburnums, chokeberry (*Aronia*), and others, and work well with grasses and peonies. Lilies make fine companion plants in the sunny border. They are often grown alone in lily beds. —*CL*

Lycoris squamigera

AUGUST LILY, LORDS AND LADIES, NAKED LADY, SURPRISE LILY

The wide, strap-like foliage of *Lycoris* emerges in early spring, only to fade away by midsummer before flowers emerge. Then—like magic—the buds pop up on naked stems in August. Clusters of five to seven metallic, rose-pink flowers, often with a pale periwinkle blush, open and fade within a week, but the show is glorious while it lasts. Plants grow from true bulbs with long, slender necks.

NATIVE HABITAT Meadows and scrublands in Japan

HARDINESS ZONES 4 to 9

HOW TO GROW Set bulbs in the garden in summer or early autumn, with the nose several inches below the soil. Plants often lie dormant the first season, and seldom bloom for two years after planting. Give them rich, moist but well-drained soil in a spot with full sun or partial shade. Spring sunlight is essential, but these summer-dormant bulbs can thrive under deciduous trees that leaf out after the bulbs have soaked up the sun.

Spring sunlight is essential for August lilies. They do well under deciduous trees that leaf out after the bulbs have soaked up the sun at the start of the season.

CULTIVARS AND RELATED SPECIES
Golden spider lily (*L. aurea*) has clusters of rich yellow flowers with narrow, recurved tepals (petal-like structures) and protruding stamens (the male flower parts) on naked stalks in early autumn. Unlike naked ladies, the thin, strap-like foliage is produced after flowering, and persists through winter and into summer (Zones 8 to 10). Red spider lily (*L. radiata*) is a dramatic bulb with naked, 1-foot stalks topped with whorls of rosy red flowers sporting long, protruding stamens like cat's whiskers. Flowers pop out of the ground in late summer, and bloom for several weeks. The foliage follows the flowers (Zones 7 to 10).

COMPANION PLANTS Southern tradition dictates a generous drift or two of naked ladies dotted in a ground-cover of ivy or periwinkle. For more pizzazz, place clusters of bulbs in beds and borders with summer perennials like border phlox, Russian sage (*Perovskia*), and coneflowers. In a lightly shaded spot, plant them with ferns, white wood aster (*Aster divaricatus*), and Japanese anemones (*Anemone* × *hybrida*) amongst a groundcover of barrenwort (*Epimedium*). Create a backdrop for your planting with fruiting shrubs such as viburnum, dogwood, and chokeberry (*Aronia*). —*CB*

Ornithogalum saundersiae
CHINKS, CHINKERINCHEE

The common names of *Ornithogalum* come from the sound supposedly made by wind blowing through fields of dried plants. *O. saundersiae* grows easily, reaches to 4 feet on strong stems, and has excellent staying power—both on the plant and as a cut flower. The milky white flowers have open cups with pointed edges and display a prominent dark olive-green center; they cluster at the top of the stem. This summer bulb will win few beauty contests; it would be more aptly described as "interesting" than as "pretty." But it is a strong, long-lasting presence in the garden in high summer, and is an excellent addition to the vase as well.

NATIVE HABITAT The summer-rainfall (northeast) region of South Africa

HARDINESS ZONES 7 to 9

HOW TO GROW Easily grown in most garden soils, *Ornithogalum* prefers full sun and well-drained soil. It is tender and should be lifted in areas with hard frosts that freeze the ground, which includes most northern states and Canada. This species is somewhat susceptible to a variety of viral diseases and thrips. If a viral disease is suspected—that is, if the foliage is strangely mottled—destroy the plants. The species multiplies rapidly from offsets on the mother bulb; this is the easiest way to increase stock.

CULTIVARS AND RELATED SPECIES No known cultivars

COMPANION PLANTS The milky-whiteness of *O. saundersiae* blends seamlessly with other border plants and the species adds a vertical accent and touch of "coolness" to the garden in high summer.   —*SC*

Chinks are a strong, long-lasting presence in the garden in high summer and an excellent addition to the vase.

Pardanthopsis dichotoma
VESPER IRIS

This member of the iris family is worth every effort to please. Its fragrant, medium blue or greenish white flowers are spotted or streaked with lilac-purple; the flowers, held on branched stems about 3 feet high above blue-gray, fan-like leaves, open at dusk and close at dawn from late summer until well into fall.

NATIVE HABITAT Full sun in scrub and grassy places in China, Japan, and Russia

HARDINESS ZONES 7 to 10

HOW TO GROW Vesper iris is short-lived even when happy, so it is important to collect and sow seeds

The creamy white flowers of tuberoses have a sweet scent.

each year. The slender seed capsules ripen in late fall but are best held and sown early the following spring, eliminating the difficulty of winter survival. In winter the plants disappear almost completely, coming back into growth in early spring. Vesper irises grow well in sun or light shade but require excellent drainage.

CULTIVARS AND RELATED SPECIES
Pardanthopsis has been crossed with *Belamcanda*, resulting in the "candy lily," × *Pardancanda norrisii*. The flowers of this hybrid plant often have purplish and orange tints. Its requirements are the same as those of the parents.

COMPANION PLANTS Vesper iris looks good with asters, late-blooming salvias, and roses. It is best planted near an entrance to the house or by a porch where the flowers can be seen in early evening and their delicate scent appreciated.   *—NG*

Polianthes tuberosa
TUBEROSE

The sweet scent of summer's tuberoses is not soon forgotten. The creamy white tubular flowers, like waxen stars, open in succession in summer for a month or more on narrow, 2-foot stalks. Grassy basal leaves are produced with the flowers, and must be left to ripen after the flowers fade. The flowers hold well when cut, so bring some of the bounty and perfume indoors.

NATIVE HABITAT The genus is native to Mexico, though this species is not known in the wild; it is likely of garden origin.

HARDINESS ZONES 8 to 10

HOW TO GROW Set out tuberoses in spring after the ground warms up, about an inch below the soil surface. If you soak the rhizomes for 12 hours before planting, they will kick into growth faster. Plants thrive in humus-rich, moist soil in full sun or light shade. Too much shade will make the stems flop, ruining the display. Where summer is short, start the bulbs indoors in moist potting soil, and set them out after the last frost date. Lift the bulbs in autumn after flowering and before frost. Store the bulbs dry in a cool but not cold place.

CULTIVARS AND RELATED SPECIES 'Single Mexican' is a popular selection with single flowers. It's easy to understand the popularity of double-flowered 'The Pearl': Each flower is like a corsage. 'Marginata' is stunning, with cream-edged foliage and single flowers on 1-foot stalks.

COMPANION PLANTS Mix drifts of three to five bulbs throughout a sunny bed. The ghostly flowers and seductive scent are perfect additions to a garden designed for evening revelry. Suitable companions in an evening garden include white peonies and border phlox, as well as baby's breath, bowman's root (*Porteranthus trifoliatus,* also known as *Gillenia trifoliata*), and Mongolian aster (*Asteromoea mongolica*). In a garden of mixed colors, try catmint, salvias, bee balm, and roses. —*CB*

Sandersonia aurantiaca

CHINESE LANTERN LILY, CHRISTMAS BELLS

This genus, whose name derives from John Sanderson, honorary secretary of the Horticultural Society of Natal, South Africa, in the 19th century, is represented by a single species, *S. aurantiaca*. This scrambling plant climbs by means of tendril-tipped leaves to a height of 2 to 2½ feet. The flowers are produced singly in the upper leaf axils. Hanging by their inch-long pedicels (flower stems), they strongly resemble Chinese lanterns and are a lovely shade of tawny orange. They are delightful, especially to children.

NATIVE HABITAT Eastern Cape region of South Africa

HARDINESS ZONES 8 to 10

HOW TO GROW *Sandersonia* is a summer grower and bloomer; since it hails from the Southern Hemisphere, its summer bloom occurs in December, thus its common name, Christmas bells. Do not let this confuse you: In the North, these plants (which grow from a fragile stoloniferous corm) must be planted in spring and can be expected to bloom in July or August. Christmas bells are best used as container plants because they are not robust. Handle the two-lobed corms gingerly and pot in a rich but extremely well drained mix. Severe frost and winter wet are lethal, two more reasons to grow this plant in a container that can be stored in a cool, dry, and frost-free location. Provide it with bamboo stakes or a

The scrambling Chinese lantern lily climbs by means of tendril-tipped leaves. Provide support with bamboo stakes or a pot trellis put in place at planting time.

pot trellis to climb. Propagate by division or seed. Seed germination is notoriously erratic; sown deeply in March in a seed tray, just a few may germinate, or none at all until the second year. Seed is viable up to five years, so seedlings may appear a few at a time for years. Once germination has taken place, growth is fast, and you can expect bloom in the second season. In any case, the corms do not seem to be long-lived in cultivation, so be ready to replace your plants every couple of years. Do not let this keep you from trying this exotic charmer! Just keep in mind that *all parts of this plant are toxic*!

CULTIVARS AND RELATED SPECIES
None
COMPANION PLANTS *Sandersonia* is best handled in a container or as a specimen plant; it can be lovely scrambling over neighboring plants. *—SC*

Sauromatum venosum
VOODOO LILY

Sauromatum's flowers don't smell good to people, but they are very attractive to flies, gnats, and other insects necessary to the plant's pollination. This aroid is most similar to Jack-in-the-pulpit, with both male and female flowers growing along a spadix surrounded and covered by a purple or green spathe. The interior of this spathe, the showy part of the flower, has a purple-spotted, lizard-like surface. After flowering ceases a large, handsome leaf composed of a horizontal fan of leaflets is borne on a thick, green stem well marked with blotches of purple.

NATIVE HABITAT Moist, shady sites in northwest India

HARDINESS ZONES 7 to 10

HOW TO GROW Voodoo lily grows best in shade. Although it's hardy at least to Zone 7, it seldom blooms if left in the ground over winter. Dig the tubers when the leaves begin to shrivel in fall and store them dry in a cool basement or greenhouse. Plants will come into growth on their own when the temperature begins to rise, and will even bloom with no soil. Voodoo lilies are best planted away from the house, because of the foul odor of the flowers. They grow easily in pots sunk to their rims in soil. You can grow them from seed, but they are most easily increased by pulling off the small oval growths that form along the edge of the main tuber.

CULTIVARS AND RELATED SPECIES No cultivars. *S. nubicum*, the only other species in the genus, is probably not available commercially.

COMPANION PLANTS Sauromatums are attractive foliage plants growing near hellebores, or at the base of mahonias or other shade-loving shrubs.   *—NG*

Scadoxus species
BLOOD LILY

Scadoxus was at one time included in the genus *Haemanthus*, but is now considered distinct for several reasons: *Haemanthus* has true bulbs and fleshy leaves, whereas *Scadoxus* is rhizomatous and produces thin leaves with a distinct midrib.

Haemanthus produces two leaves per year, which persist for more than a year in the evergreen species. *Scadoxus* produces up to nine leaves, usually in a whorl, and in several species the leaf bases clasp to form a pseudostem. This botanical clarity has not been followed in the horticultural world, and, as with the confusion surrounding the plants in genera *Gloxinia/Siningia* and *Amaryllis/Hippeastrum*, the confusion about *Scadoxus* can be expected to persist indefinitely. Since some truly remarkable plants can be found in both genera, and since most of what is offered commercially is summer-growing or evergreen, I counsel boldness: Give these plants a try!

The flowers of the voodoo lily give off a foul odor, so it's best to plant it away from the house.

NATIVE HABITAT Tropical to southern Africa

HARDINESS ZONES 8 to 10

HOW TO GROW Plant shallowly in a rich, well-drained mix. Depending on species, up to one-half of the spotted ornamental bulb may be left exposed above soil level. Evergreen varieties need some shade from midday sun, whereas deciduous varieties like a brighter, but not sun-baked, position. All require moderate yet consistent water when in leaf. A weak, general-purpose fertilizer, either granular or liquid, is suitable for these moderate feeders. Depending on variety and culture, it is possible to have *Scadoxus* in flower from mid-spring to early winter; pot culture extends their summer usefulness to most parts of the U.S.

CULTIVARS AND RELATED SPECIES Note the botanical/horticultural confusion described above.

COMPANION PLANTS Most *Scadoxus/Haemanthus* are best used in containers as specimen plants.   —*SC*

Schizostylis coccinea
CRIMSON FLAG

Brilliant sunset colors as well as the softer shades of dawn characterize the late-season flowers of crimson flag. The starry, six-petaled flowers open up in late summer and autumn on slender stalks reminiscent of delicate *Gladiolus* spires. Plants produce abundant, sword-like leaves from slender rhizomes, and multiply generously to form thick, multi-flowered clumps.

NATIVE HABITAT South Africa

Depending on variety and culture, it is possible to have blood lily in flower from mid-spring to early winter. Above is *Scadoxus multiflorus* subspecies *katherinae*.

In late summer and autumn, the starry flowers of crimson flag open on slender stalks. Plants multiply generously to form thick, multi-flowered clumps.

HARDINESS ZONES 5 (with winter protection) to 10

HOW TO GROW Crimson flags are easy to grow in pots or in the ground. Give containerized plants a light but rich, well-drained soil, place the container in a sunny spot, and enjoy the show. Overwinter the pots on the dry side in a cool spot. In the ground, choose a sunny to lightly shaded spot with rich, consistently moist soil. Foliage will emerge early in the spring, and flowering will start in August and continue through October in the north, later in warmer zones.

CULTIVARS AND RELATED SPECIES The undisputed king of crimson flag colors is 'Oregon Sunset', whose intense cerise flowers glow in the evening light. 'Salmon Charm' is rosy salmon, while 'Sunrise' is deep pink. 'Mrs. Hegarty' and 'November Cheer' are autumn-flowering pure pinks, while 'Viscountess Byng' is a softer shell pink and the last to flower. 'Alba' is pure white.

COMPANION PLANTS Match crimson flag color for color in formal or informal garden schemes. Place vibrant 'Oregon Sunset' with rich, lavender-purple aromatic aster (*Aster oblongifolius* or *Symphiotrichum oblongifolius* 'Raydon's Favorite') or royal purple New England aster (*A. novae-angliae* 'Purple Dome'). Softer shades combine well with any late-season asters, autumn sage, goldenrods, rain lilies (*Zephyranthes*), gentians, and ornamental grasses. The colorful berries of viburnums, deciduous hollies, and beautyberry (*Callicarpa*) add to the show.   —*CB*

Scilla scilloides, above, has pinker blooms on taller stalks than *Scilla autumnalis*, and flowers later.

Scilla autumnalis
AUTUMN SQUILL

The genus *Scilla* is most often associated with spring, but the bloom of this species reaches its peak in July and August. It is seldom out of sight, for new flowers appear just as the previous season's leaves disappear in summer. Relatively large bulbs (poisonous in some species) produce stalks bearing up to 16 small white, lilac, or purple flowers in midsummer. Slender, dark green leaves appear in fall and persist throughout winter. This scilla has been described as not showy enough for most gardeners, but when grown in large numbers, I believe it makes a wonderful display.

NATIVE HABITAT Deciduous woods or sun from Great Britain to Turkey

HARDINESS ZONES 6 to 9

HOW TO GROW This species will self-sow if grown well. It's also easy to collect seeds and sow them in a small flat to grow through the winter and plant out in fall. They will bloom a year or two after sowing. Autumn squill grows easily in shade, and is drought tolerant.

CULTIVARS AND RELATED SPECIES *S. scilloides,* with pinker flowers on taller stalks, begins to bloom in August but its main display is later in fall.

COMPANION PLANTS Autumn squill's flowers persist into fall, so combine it with fall-flowering *Cyclamen mirabile, C. hederifolium,* and *C. cilicium.*   —*NG*

Sternbergia lutea

WINTER DAFFODIL, AUTUMN CROCUS

Golden yellow chalices spring leafless and naked from bare ground to bid farewell to the last days of summer. The 6 colorful tepals (petal-like flower structures) bring the light of the setting sun into the garden through the autumn. Long, grass-like foliage is produced in autumn, after the flowers fade, and persists right through the winter until early summer, when it discreetly fades away. Plants grow from true bulbs.

NATIVE HABITAT Meadows and open woods throughout Southern Europe to Central Asia

HARDINESS ZONES 6 to 10

HOW TO GROW *Sternbergia* thrives in any good, well-drained soil in full sun to partial shade. Set out dormant bulbs in summer with the nose of the bulb 2 inches below the soil surface. Plants will bloom the first season, and will quickly multiply into floriferous clumps. If the clumps get too thick, bloom declines. Lift tangled clumps in spring before the foliage fades and gently tease the bulbs apart. Replant in enriched soil. This plant is in high demand and short supply, so order early to avoid heartbreak.

CULTIVARS AND RELATED SPECIES 'Major' is a surprisingly scarce cultivar, but worth seeking for its larger flowers and wider foliage.

COMPANION PLANTS Complement the golden color of this late-summer beauty with golden-leafed companions. Place a generous drift of bulbs where they can pop up through a groundcover of golden thyme or golden marjoram, or a combination of the two. Yellow-flowered autumn sage (*Salvia greggii* 'Moonlight') will add height to the planting, backed by a golden-leafed elderberry (*Sambucus canadensis* 'Aurea'). For contrast, add a few bulbs of red spider lily (*Lycoris radiata*) against a complementary backdrop of magenta autumn sage (*Salvia* 'Maraschino') and the effect is riveting. To extend the season, add some spring-blooming, yellow-flowered *Crocus chrysanthus*. —*CB*

Plant winter daffodil in summer and it will bloom in its first season.

Given enough moisture, tiger flowers open from midsummer on. Each flower is up to 5 inches in diameter and lasts only one day.

Tigridia pavonia

TIGER FLOWER, MEXICAN SHELL FLOWER

Tigridia is one of summer's stars. From midsummer on, spectacular cupped flowers with outspread petals open whenever there is enough moisture. Each flower, which lasts but a day, is up to 5 inches in diameter and can be white, yellow, lilac, rose, or red, with or without spots. The flowers have six tepals (petal-like structures)— three large outer tepals and three much smaller inner ones—that come together at their base to form a shell-like cup. The plant gets its common names for its markings and shape, but its species name, *pavonia,* is more apt. The flower is as brilliant as a peacock. The plants grow from corms and produce pleated, green iris-like leaves to about 18 inches long.

NATIVE HABITAT Sunny areas in Mexico and Central America

HARDINESS ZONES 7 to 10 (in colder areas it will survive with a thick mulch)

HOW TO GROW Tigridias like full sun and well-drained soil. Although books recommend sandy soil, tigridias tolerate clay as well. They are easily propagated from seed sown in spring and from division of the small corms that grow near well-developed plants. In colder areas lift the corms in fall to ensure their survival.

CULTIVARS AND RELATED SPECIES 'Grandiflora' has large flowers. Other cultivar names indicate color:

'Alba' is white; 'Lutea' is yellow; 'Aurea' has yellow petals with centers spotted in red; 'Canariensis' is pale yellow, with centers spotted in red; 'Carminia' is pinkish red with darker spots.

COMPANION PLANTS *Tigridia* looks good with summer-flowering shrubs such as vitex or coming up through verbenas.   —*NG*

Triteleia (Brodiaea) laxa
TRIPLET LILY

Good things come in small packages. Diminutive, chocolate-colored bulbs give rise to slender, grassy foliage and a wealth of flowers that dance in the breeze on wiry stems. The slender 2-foot stems are crowned with open umbels of up-facing, starry chalices in a delicious shade of blue. Plants are exquisite in the garden, and their staying power has made them an indispensable cut flower.

NATIVE HABITAT Open woods, chaparral, and desert scrub in western North America

HARDINESS ZONES 5 to 9

HOW TO GROW Place bulbs in rich, evenly moist, well-drained soil in full sun to light shade. Plants are native to arid regions, so the soil can become dry after the flowers fade. Bulbs of this short-lived perennial are inexpensive, so replant them each fall to assure bloom where they are unreliably hardy, or when they refuse to become established as perennials. The foliage appears early, and often disappears before the flowers emerge. Mix the bulbs

Purple triplet lily provides support for twining *Dichelostemma volubile.*

among other plants so you do not inadvertently dig into them.

CULTIVARS AND RELATED SPECIES 'Corrina' has lovely violet-blue flowers, while those of 'Queen Fabiola' are rich indigo. Pretty face (*T. ixioides* 'Starlight') has fat umbels of rich, buttermilk-yellow flowers in late spring and early summer on 1½-foot stems (Zones 5 to 9).

COMPANION PLANTS Triplet lilies are easy to work into a garden scheme. Their bright blue color harmonizes with pinks, soft yellows, and whites, and you can create some startling contrasts by combining them with orange and red flowers. Combine them, too, with billowing plants like bowman's root

(*Porteranthus trifoliatus,* also known as *Gillenia trifoliata*) and sea lavender (*Limonium latifolium*) so the flowers seem to float in an airy cloud of color. Other good companions include pinks (*Dianthus*), phlox, catmint, sages, and free-seeding annuals like love-in-a-mist (*Nigella*) and Bishop's flower (*Ammi majus*).   —*CB*

Tulbaghia violacea
TULBAGHIA

A member of the allium family, *Tulbaghia* has the expected oniony fragrance in its foliage. It is among the most useful of all summer-flowering bulbs, blooming from early June until frost with umbels of

Tulbaghias need little from the gardener except good soil and full sun.

lavender-blue flowers on stalks about 15 inches high. The leaves of *Tulbaghia violacea* are gray-green and blade-like.

NATIVE HABITAT Sunny sites in South Africa

HARDINESS ZONES Zone 7 to 10

HOW TO GROW *Tulbaghia* needs little from the grower except good garden soil and full sun. It is drought-tolerant, surviving heat, humidity, and extended periods without rain. Several tender species are worth growing in pots in northern regions; protect them from winter frost in a cool greenhouse.

CULTIVARS AND RELATED SPECIES *T. v. pallida* is an elegant, white-flowered form of the species plant. The flowers are held on shorter stalks, but the blooming period is as long as its cousin's. The variegated foliage of *T. v.* 'Silver Lace' is reason enough to grow it. This form is not as vigorous as the others but worth the extra effort to sustain. The smaller species, *T. cepacea,* has all of the advantages of its larger cousin. It remains only 12 inches high and is beautiful growing at the edge of the border. All are hardy from Zones 7 to 10. Tender *T. simmleri* (Zone 8) blooms from late summer into fall. The foliage is broader than that of the other species and the flowers are produced on stalks more than 2 feet high.

COMPANION PLANTS Tulbaghias are beautiful with yuccas, bloody cranesbill (*Geranium sanguineum*), veronicas, and *Saponaria* × *lempergii* 'Max Frei'.   —*NG*

Most rain lilies are native to areas with hot summers and can withstand lengthy droughts, coming into growth and flowering when rains resume. Above is *Zephyranthes candida*.

Zephyranthes species
RAIN LILY, FAIRY LILY, ZEPHYR LILY

From spring into fall, one or more species of this star of the summer-flowering bulbs genera blooms, bearing lily-like flowers held vertically at the top of the stalks above bladelike foliage.

NATIVE HABITAT Sunny or lightly shaded areas in South and Central America, Mexico, and the southern U.S.

HARDINESS ZONES 7 to 10

HOW TO GROW Most rain lilies grow best in well-drained soil in the sun, and need water to bloom well. I have read that they prefer sand to clay and that the soil should be nearly neutral. I grow mine in clay loam but give most of them sunny locations. I add a little lime to those grown in pots. Late summer-flowering *Z. candida*, with its pure white flowers, is probably the hardiest species, but I can vouch only for those growing in my Zone 7 climate. Most of these plants are native to areas with hot summers and can withstand lengthy droughts, coming into growth and flowering when rainfall is adequate.

CULTIVARS AND RELATED SPECIES *Z. citrina* seems to bloom on cue, producing successive flushes of flowers throughout the summer. Dozens of flowers open on the same day and several weeks later they all do it again. Green leaves have tinges of red-brown near their base, but the flowers are pure yellow.

Golden-yellow *Z. flavissima* blooms earlier than most of its cousins, and flowers appear throughout summer, producing seeds above ground while the bulbs multiply below. This rain lily survives near-zero temperatures. *Z.* 'Capricorn' has burgundy buds and a spathe with burgundy stripes. The flower opens wide to reveal interior petals with burgundy stripes over a pale yellow base. The petals shade to green on both sides. *Z.* 'La Buffa Rose' is one of the most elegant rain lilies, with upfacing pink or white with pink flowers. The broad outer sepals seem to form a base for the narrower inner petals. Its cousin, *Z. morrisclintii,* has smaller, white flowers tinged with pink. *Z. macrosiphon* has a dark burgundy spathe covering the bud. This covering folds back as the flower opens to reveal deep rose-pink petals shaded to white in the interior. This species blooms again and again throughout summer. *Z. grandiflora* is similar to the preceding one but with paler pink, slightly crepey petals. This rain lily is generally sterile, but occasionally I get a seedpod that I promptly sow. The exquisite pure white, fragrant flowers of *Z. drummondii* (also known as *Cooperia pedunculata*) open in the afternoon at the tops of long perianth tubes. This species needs lime. The similar *Z. traubii,* also white, blooms in late September. The narrow exterior petals of *Z. commersoniana* are white flushed with pink. The interior of the flower has slender lines that lead to a green throat. *Z. lancasterae* is another white-flowered, long-blooming *Zephyranthes* with petals flushed with pink. Some of the most beautiful rain lilies are pale yellow. *Z. smallii* has primrose yellow, scentless flowers. Stalk after stalk, each bearing only one flower, appear throughout summer. This species must be increased through seeds; it doesn't multiply underground. In cool weather, each flower will last several days. *Z. reginae* also produces clear, pale yellow flowers off and on all summer long.

COMPANION PLANTS Plant *Z. flavissima* with dark purple verbenas. *Z. citrina* is beautiful with buddleias. *Z.* 'Capricorn' is good with red salvias and burgundy grasses. *Z.* 'Labuffarosea' is attractive with pink-flowered lespedezas. The white species *Z. morrisclintii, Z. commersoniana, Z. candida,* and *Z. lancasterae* (*Z. drumondii* × *grandiflora*) look good with magenta petunias and violet verbenas. Deep pink *Z. macrosiphon* is beautiful with white verbenas and mauve *Allium senescens*. Primrose yellow *Z. smallii* and *Z. reginae* look attractive coming up through dark burgundy *Sedum spurium* 'Feldglut'. *Z. grandiflora* is beautiful growing near *Tradescantia pallida* 'Purple Heart'. —*NG* 🎔

USDA HARDINESS ZONE MAP

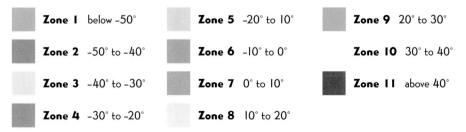

ZONES & MINIMUM WINTER TEMPERATURES (°F.)

Zone 1 below –50°	**Zone 5** –20° to 10°	**Zone 9** 20° to 30°
Zone 2 –50° to –40°	**Zone 6** –10° to 0°	**Zone 10** 30° to 40°
Zone 3 –40° to –30°	**Zone 7** 0° to 10°	**Zone 11** above 40°
Zone 4 –30° to –20°	**Zone 8** 10° to 20°	

SUPPLIERS

BULBS

ANTONELLI BROTHERS
2545 Capitola Road
Santa Cruz, CA 95062
831-475-5222
831-475-7066 fax
www.antnelli.com

BRENT AND BECKY'S BULBS
7463 Heath Trail
Gloucester, VA 23061
877-661-2852, 804-693-3966
804-693-9436 fax
www.brentandbeckysbulbs.com

B&D LILIES
P.O. Box 2007
Port Townsend, WA 98368
360-765-4342
360-765-4074 fax
www.bdlilies.com

DUTCH GARDENS
P.O. Box 2037
Lakewood, NJ 08701
800-818-3861
www.dutchgardens.com

ADAMS EDEN NURSERY
15321 N.W. State Road 121
Gainesville, FL 32653
904-418-0484
www.4view.com/adams_eden

LOGEE'S GREENHOUSES
141 North Street
Danielson, CT 06239-1939
888-330-8038, 860-774-8038
888-774-9932 fax
www.logees.com

McCLURE & ZIMMERMAN
108 W. Winnebago St.
P.O. Box 368
Friesland, WI 53935-0368
800-883-6998
800-374-6120 fax
www.mzbulb.com

MESSELAAR BULB CO.
160 County Road, Route 1A
P.O. Box 269
Ipswich, MA 01938
978-356-3737
www.tulipbulbs.com

ODYSSEY BULBS
8984 Meadow Lane
Berrien Springs, MI 49103
616-471-4642 (also fax)
www.odysseybulbs.com

OLD HOUSE GARDENS
536 W. Third St.
Ann Arbor, MI 48103-4957
734-995-1486
734-995-1687 fax
www.oldhousegardens.com

PLANT DELIGHTS NURSERY
9241 Sauls Road
Raleigh, NC 27603
919-772-4794
919-662-0370 fax
www.plantdelights.com

SINGING SPRINGS NURSERY
8802 Wilderson Road
Cedar Grove, NC 27231-9324
919-732-9403
919-732-6336 fax

VAN BOURGONDIEN
P.O. Box 1000
Babylon, NY 11702
800-622-9997
800-327-4268 fax
www.dutchbulbs.com

WAYSIDE GARDENS
1 Garden Lane
Hodges, SC 29695
800-845-1124
800-817-1124 fax
www.waysidegardens.com

YUCCA DO NURSERY
P.O. Box 907
Hempstead, TX 77445
979-826-4580
www.yuccado.com

ENVIRONMENTALLY SOUND PEST AND DISEASE CONTROLS

GARDENS ALIVE
5100 Schenley Place
Lawrenceburg, IN 47025
812-537-8650
812-537-5108 fax
www.gardensalive.com

ARBICO
P.O. Box 8910
Tucson, AZ 85738
800-827-2847, 520-825-9785
520-825-2038 fax
www.arbico.com

RINCON-VITOVA INSECTARIES
P.O. Box 1555
Ventura, CA 93002-1555
800-248-2847
805-643-6267 fax
www.rinconvitova.com

FOR MORE INFORMATION

NATURALIZING BULBS
Rob Proctor
Henry Holt and Company, 1997

THE COMPLETE BOOK OF BULBS, CORMS, TUBERS, AND RHIZOMES: A STEP-BY-STEP GUIDE TO NATURE'S EASIEST AND MOST REWARDING PLANTS
Brian Mathew & Philip Swindells
Reader's Digest, 1994

GROWING BULBS: THE COMPLETE PRACTICAL GUIDE
Brian Mathew
Timber Press, 1997

PERENNIALS FOR TODAY'S GARDENS
C. Colston Burrell
Meredith Books, 2000

CONTRIBUTORS

C. COLSTON BURRELL is an avid plantsman, garden designer, and award-winning author. His books include *Perennials for Today's Gardens; Perennial Combinations,* a Garden Book Club best-seller; and *A Gardener's Encyclopedia of Wildflowers,* and he is the editor of several BBG handbooks, most recently *Wildflower Gardens* (1999) and *The Shady Border* (1998). He gardens on ten acres in the Blue Ridge Mountains of Virginia.

SCOTT CANNING is a former gardener at Brooklyn Botanic Garden. He tended warm-temperate plants, including a large collection of South African bulbs, from 1994 to 1999, and was curator of the Cranford Rose Garden.

ALESSANDRO CHIARI has been the plant propagator at Brooklyn Botanic Garden since 1998. He studied tropical agriculture at the University of Florence, Italy, and plant science at the University of Connecticut, and has worked as a horticulturist in Zambia, Paraguay, Chile, and Peru.

STEVEN E. CLEMANTS is vice-president for science and publications at Brooklyn Botanic Garden, co-director of the Center for Urban Restoration Ecology (CURE), and past coordinator of BBG's New York Metropolitan Flora (NYMF). He has published articles in several BBG handbooks as well as numerous scientific papers.

JACKIE FAZIO is the director of horticulture at Brooklyn Botanic Garden. She has been teaching pest management techniques in the BBG Continuing Education Department's Certificate in Horticulture program since 1995, and has been overseeing pest management on the BBG grounds since 1994.

NANCY GOODWIN is a gardener at Montrose, in Hillsborough, North Carolina. She is co-author with Allen Lacy of *A Year in Our Gardens: Letters by Nancy Goodwin and Allen Lacy* (University Press of North Carolina, 2001).

BETH HANSON is former managing editor of the Brooklyn Botanic Garden's *21st-Century Gardening Series.* She is the editor of the BBG handbooks *Easy Compost* (1997), *Chile Peppers* (1999), *Natural Disease Control* (2000), and *Gourmet Herbs* (2001), and contributed to *The Brooklyn Botanic Garden Gardener's Desk Reference* (Henry Holt, 1998). She lives outside New York City and writes about gardening, health, and the environment for various publications.

BRENT AND BECKY HEATH are garden educators who own and operate "Brent and Becky's Bulbs," a wholesale/retail catalogue and web-site flower-bulb business in Gloucester, Virginia. They distribute all types of bulbs to gardeners, cities, universities, and botanical gardens throughout the United States. Daffodil hybridizers, Brent and Becky are co-authors of *Daffodils for American Gardens.* They received the American Horticultural Society's Gold Medal in 2001.

CHUCK LEVINE is a professional horticulturist as well as a teacher of horticulture and botany for the Minnesota State Horticulture Society, Intermediate School District #287, and Hennepin Technical College. He has worked as a horticulture specialist for the Chicago Botanic Garden and the Minnesota Extension Service, and developed and implemented a curriculum on vocational plant production for the Hennepin County Corrections Facility in Plymouth, Minnesota. Chuck's own acre of urban paradise is in Roseville, Minnesota.

TOVAH MARTIN is the author of several books on gardening, including *Tasha Tudor's Garden, Garden Whimsy,* and *Heirloom Flowers.* Her most recent book is *A Time to Blossom: Mothers, Daughters & Flowers* (2001). She lives and gardens in containers and otherwise in the Litchfield Hills of Connecticut with her Maine coon cat and goats.

CHRISTOPHER S. ROBBINS is a senior program officer at TRAFFIC North America of World Wildlife Fund-US who specializes in plant trade and conservation.

ILLUSTRATIONS AND PHOTOS

Bulb and critter illustrations by **STEVE BUCHANAN**
DAVID CAVAGNARO cover, pages 1, 4, 6, 15, 16, 17, 18, 19, 21, 28, 29, 30, 37, 38, 39, 47, 53, 56, 58, 60, 61, 67, 69, 71, 80, 82, 83, 84, 88, 97, 99
BECKY & BRENT HEATH pages 5, 24, 25, 26, 27, 31, 40, 50, 54, 55, 64, 65, 70, 72, 74, 76, 77, 81, 86, 90, 91, 94
DEREK FELL pages 8, 9, 22, 23, 59, 75, 96
ALESSANDRO CHIARI page 12 (top and bottom)
ALAN & LINDA DETRICK pages 43, 78, 95, 98
JERRY PAVIA pages 48, 51, 63, 73, 87, 92, 93
NEW ENGLAND WILDFLOWER SOCIETY page 57

INDEX

BROOKLYN BOTANIC GARDEN

More Books on Beautiful Bloomers

Brooklyn Botanic Garden
circa 1930

JOIN THE
BROOKLYN BOTANIC GARDEN
OR **GIVE** A GIFT
OF MEMBERSHIP

Here are the membership benefits you can enjoy and share with others:

SUBSCRIBER $35
- Subscriptions to *21st-Century Gardening Series* handbooks and *Plants & Gardens News*
- Use of Gardener's Resource Center
- Reciprocal privileges at botanical gardens across the country

INDIVIDUAL $35
- One membership card for free individual admission
- 10% discount at the Garden Gift Shop
- Entry to members' summer hours, Sunset Picnics, and Preview Night at the Plant Sale
- Discounts on adult classes, trips, and tours
- *BBG Members News* and course catalog mailings
- Use of Gardener's Resource Center
- Reciprocal privileges at botanical gardens across the country

FAMILY/DUAL $65
All of the above INDIVIDUAL benefits, plus
- 2 membership cards for free admission for 2 adults & their children under 16
- Free parking for 4 visits
- 10% discount at the Terrace Cafe
- Discounts on children's programs and classes
- Subscriptions to *21st-Century Gardening Series* handbooks and *Plants & Gardens News*

FAMILY/DUAL PLUS $95
All of the above, plus
- 1 guest admitted free each time you come
- Free parking for 8 visits
- 2 SUBSCRIBER gift memberships for the price of one

SIGNATURE $150
All of the above, plus
- Your choice of one Signature Plant
- Free parking for 12 visits
- A special BBG gift calendar

SPONSOR $300
All of the above, plus
- Your choice of 2 Signature Plants
- 4 complimentary one-time guest passes
- Free parking for 18 visits

PATRON $500
All of the above, plus
- 2 guests admitted free each time you come
- Recognition in selected printed materials
- Free parking for 24 visits

GAGER SOCIETY $1500
All of the above, plus
- Unlimited free guests each time you come
- Gager Society Dinner and garden trip
- Complimentary INDIVIDUAL gift membership for a friend
- Private receptions for higher level donors
- Unlimited free parking for a year

Please use the form on reverse to join.
For more information, call the Membership Department: 718-623-7210

MEMBERSHIP FORM

Your Name

Address

City   State   Zip   Membership #

Daytime phone   Evening phone

email   ☐ Check if this is a renewal.

Please enroll me as a member of the Brooklyn Botanic Garden.

☐ Subscriber $35   ☐ Signature $150
☐ Individual $35   ☐ Sponsor $300
☐ Family/Dual $65   ☐ Patron $500
☐ Family/Dual Plus $95   ☐ Gager Society $1500

Please send a gift membership to the recipient below.

☐ Subscriber $35   ☐ Signature $150
☐ Individual $35   ☐ Sponsor $300
☐ Family/Dual $65   ☐ Patron $500
☐ Family/Dual Plus $95   ☐ Gager Society $1500

Gift Recipient's Name

Address

City   State   Zip

Daytime phone   Evening phone

email

Method of Payment

☐ Check (payable to Brooklyn Botanic Garden)
☐ Visa ☐ MasterCard ☐ AMEX

Card #   Exp. Date

Signature

Please tear along perforation, complete form and return with payment to:
Membership Office, Brooklyn Botanic Garden,
1000 Washington Avenue, Brooklyn, NY 11225-1099
Phone: 718-623-7210 Fax: 718-857-2430